KAWARTHAS NATURE

KAWARTHAS NATURE

Compiled by The Peterborough Field Naturalists

Stoddart · A BOSTON MILLS PRESS BOOK

Canadian Cataloguing in Publication Data

Main entry under title:

Kawarthas nature

Includes bibliographical references.
ISBN 1-55046-058-7

1. Natural history – Ontario – Kawartha Lakes
Region – Guidebooks. 2. Kawartha Lakes Region
(Ont.) – Description and travel. 3. Trails –
Ontario – Kawartha Lakes Region – Guidebooks.
4. Natural areas – Ontario – Kawartha Lakes Region –
Guidebooks. I. Nugent, E. A. II. Peterborough
Field Naturalists.

QH106.2.05K3 1992   508.713'67   C92-093917-1

First published in 1992 by
Stoddart Publishing Co. Limited
34 Lesmill Road
Toronto, Canada
M3B 2T6

A Boston Mills Press Book
The Boston Mills Press
132 Main Street
Erin, Ontario
N0B 1T0

Winners of the
Heritage Canada
Communications Award

American Association
for State and Local History
Award of Merit

Design by Gillian Stead and Mary Firth
Edited by Noel Hudson
Typography by Justified Type Inc., Guelph, Ontario
Printed in Canada

The publisher gratefully acknowledges the support of The Canada Council,
Ontario Arts Council and Ontario Publishing Centre in the development
of writing and publishing in Canada.

Back cover: Ontario Transportation Map Series, Map 7 (detail)
          Available from the Ministry of Transportation, Ontario.

TABLE OF CONTENTS

Winter

ACKNOWLEDGEMENTS

The Book Committee would like to thank all those who have contributed their time, effort and talents to make this book possible.

We would like to express our gratitude to the many contributors who have submitted articles, and to the staff of the Otonabee, Kawartha and Ganaraska Conservation Authorities and the Ministry of Natural Resources at Bancroft and Lindsay for their co-operation and assistance.

Our thanks also to the many photographers who submitted slides for our consideration, for their patience during the long selection process, and to Steve Gardiner for his excellent maps and Gordon Berry for the illustrations.

Our gratitude is also extended to John Denison of the Boston Mills Press for the support he has extended during the production of this book.

The Peterborough Field Naturalists Book Committee
Gordon Berry
Patricia Dunsire
Ted Nugent, Chairman

Woodland walk

FOREWORD
WELCOME TO THE KAWARTHAS!

We hope you will find this guide interesting and informative.

Major emphasis has been placed on brief descriptions of specific areas of natural interest which are readily accessible to the general public. Each of these describes some of the natural attractions at that site, and mention is also made of other recreational activities available.

To help you find these areas, the relevant section of Map 7 of the Ontario Transportation Map Series is reproduced on the back cover, and reference grid letters and numbers are noted near the beginning of each article. You will find this portion of the Ministry of Transportation map useful, and you may wish to obtain the full map from them.

The other major group of articles describes the landforms, wildflowers and wild animals of the entire area. They outline some of the features you may see, and how you may go about seeing them. They are intended only to offer a "taste of honey" and to whet your appetite for more information.

A list of references at the back of the book suggests guides which may be helpful when you wish to learn more.

An appendix lists other sources of information. As addresses and telephone numbers may change, it would be prudent to check the current validity of these listings in the telephone directory or with the information bureau.

Comments and amendments from readers are welcome.

We hope you will enjoy the Kawarthas as much as we do.

The Peterborough Field Naturalists,
On the occasion of their 50th Anniversary,
1940 - 1990

One touch of Nature makes the whole world kin. SHAKESPEARE

Late frost

CODE FOR TRAIL USERS

* Stay on the trail. Use only marked routes.

* Use stiles to cross fences. Close any gate behind you.

* Respect all animals, plants and trees. Protect and avoid disturbing wildlife, especially during the nesting or breeding season.

* Carry out all litter. Leave nothing but footprints, take nothing but photographs.

* Fires may only be lit at designated camping or picnic sites.

* No smoking while walking along the trails.

* Never strip bark from trees.

* Keep dogs on a leash while on or near farmland and where requested in parks.

* Respect private property at all times.

* Leave flowers and plants for others to enjoy.

* At all times behave as guests.

SUGGESTIONS FOR HIKERS

Gordon Berry

What to wear:

Light hiking boots or ankle-high running shoes with heavy soles are best for most walking trails encountered in this book. Many trails traverse uneven, rocky terrain, and ankle support is important to avoid injury. A good fit is vital to avoid chafing or blisters, and treaded, non-slip rubber or synthetic soles are safer than leather. Thick wool socks are better than thin synthetic ones. Take care of your feet; remember, they have to bring you home.

Wear light-coloured clothing. Long-sleeved shirts and full-length pants, both in loose styles which can be closed at the wrist and ankle, offer the best protection against insects in spring. Layers of clothing are better than thicker garments when warmth is required in the fall or winter. In summer, shorts and a loose-fitting top are better than tight-fitting T-shirts.

Hats are important for sun protection, especially if the brim shields the face and back of the neck. They are also useful in rain, especially for those who wear glasses, as they help to keep lenses clear. In cold weather they prevent unnecessary heat loss from the head.

What to take:

Carry as little as possible. You are out for enjoyment, not an endurance test. On longer trails, use a small day pack with comfortable shoulder straps. If you are walking regularly, consider buying a small hiker's first-aid kit. If not already included in the kit, add a piece of moleskin and an ointment for insect bites. Other items to consider, according to the weather, season and type of terrain you are likely to encounter, include rain wear, insect repellent, a whistle, camera and a small pair of binoculars. If taking food with you, keep it simple and light. Fluids are essential. Lightweight plastic containers with a refreshing drink are best. Small cardboard containers of fruit juice are also good, but remember that any containers or wrap you take in you must also take out.

While most of the routes suggested in this book are well marked and well used, it is a good habit to know exactly where you are at all times. If you like to walk regularly in areas near your home, buy some suitable topographic maps and use them. Learn to use a compass and glance at it from time to time as you walk. Take note of the direction of the sun as you start the walk and use it as a directional aid. Get used to using a map and compass on well-marked trails to gain confidence for more venturesome excursions in the future. If you intend to extend your walking to longer treks, consider taking an evening course in orienteering.

Trip planning:

Use good judgement when selecting trails. Don't start a long trail late in the day or in uncertain weather. Match the distance to be covered to the stamina of the youngest member of the party when children are along, or to the slowest or least fit member when only adults are present. Time (and the energy expended) will vary with the type of terrain, the enthusiasm of the walkers, and their fitness or experience.

11

Always allow more time than you expect it will actually take. Allow time to enjoy a view, to take pictures, to delight in the flowers, or to sit and rest when you want to. There are no prizes for the first one back. Remember, the best way to spoil the walk for everyone else in the party is to walk too fast.

Mosquitos and black-flies:

Insects can never be totally avoided, but a few suggestions can minimize their nuisance effect when on the trail.

The pleasant odours of colognes, aftershave, scented soaps and perfumes seem to attract mosquitos and black-flies. Eating bananas will also cause your skin to release an odour which mosquitos find attractive.

If you are allergic to insect bites, avoid the worst months, May and June. Carry and wear a repellent if you are affected by these bothersome creatures.

Safety:

On longer trails or on isolated routes, be sure to let someone know where you are going and when you expect to be back. This is particularly important if you like to go for walks alone. The rule for cross-country skiers is "Never ski alone" and this rule should be adopted by inexperienced walkers in unfamiliar territory.

Heatstroke can be produced by a combination of hot sun and exertion, resulting in dehydration and salt loss through perspiration. It is most likely to occur when walking in a breeze. A head covering is a must in hot weather, and it is important to carry adequate supplies of water. Do not neglect to cover the back of the neck. A light bandana is a very sensible protection.

Hypothermia is the most serious condition likely to threaten a hiker in the early spring, late fall or winter. Usually this occurs when the walker is lost overnight, falls into very cold water, or experiences chilling weather conditions. Any small first-aid book will give details of treatment for hypothermia. Most ski and camping books contain instructions on how to prevent loss of body heat. If you like the longer and more remote trails, consider photocopying these notes and carrying the instructions with your first-aid kit.

Many injuries incurred while walking are due to falls. Rocks are slippery and treacherous when wet; be especially careful of rock surfaces in rainy weather.

Persons who are subject to sunburn should carry and use an appropriate sun block.

Avoid illness due to drinking impure water. For the trails outlined in this book, carry drinking water with you. Many parks have some potable water source available. Dehydration in warm weather can be easily avoided. Be especially cautious with children.

Also avoid the itching misery of poison ivy; for information about this plant, see the separate box, page 13.

Smoking and fires:

It is illegal to smoke on the trail while walking. Smoke only at rest stops or campsites. Smokers should carry a small container for butts and ashes; a 35-millimetre film can with a little water in it is quite effective. Remember, more forests and parkland are lost by careless smokers and hikers than by any other cause. (Note that fires can be started by discarded bottles and broken glass, which magnify the

sun's rays.) Most parks ban fires, except in designated camping or picnic spots. If for any reason you do need to light a fire, keep it small. Be sure that it is on a rock or sandy surface, and pour plenty of water over the ashes before you leave the site. Sometimes a fire which appears to be out can smoulder in the humus material below the ground only to burst into flame hours, or even days, later.

Respect private property:

In this book we have tried to confine our trips to lands that are publicly owned. In a very few cases we have obtained the private landowner's permission to walk on private property. A wandering dog, curious child, or thoughtless adult can easily offend a property owner. Please respect private property and restriction signs. Treat anyone who questions your presence on the property with politeness; he or she may be the owner. Remember that landowners often have many trespassers and may have experienced vandalism, littering or even abusive language in the past, and their patience is often justifiably short. It is important to maintain good relations with these persons so that others may enjoy the privilege of using their land in the future.

Seeing wildlife:

The fewer the number of people in the group and the quieter the approach, the greater the chance of seeing wild animals. It is a good idea to consciously adopt a quieter level of talking in the woods. There is no need to compete with traffic and city noises or radios. As you develop a capacity for quietness, the brief, gentle sounds of the wood or field make themselves evident. You may wish to develop a few simple hand signals so that you can inform others in your group of the presence of some creature without using your voice and thus alerting the animal. Signs for "stop" or "wait," a signal for silence and no movement, a direction signal or sign for "bird," "animal," etc., can often mean that not just the first person in the group sees an animal, but other members of the party as well.

The chance of seeing small creatures is much greater than that of seeing large ones. Every bush abounds with insects and evidence of their activities. Take time to stop and look. Using your binoculars backwards or, better still, carrying a small 10X hand lens, you can magnify small objects and provide a display of details you would otherwise have missed.

There are guidebooks available on every nature topic imaginable. Don't try to transport a library with you. Consider one branch of nature that appeals to you and make an effort to learn one or two new species each time you go out.

Not all animals are shy, especially around campsites where even wild animals have become used to people. Two good general rules when watching or photographing animals are: make sure that the animal always has an escape route available, and never get between an adult animal and its young.

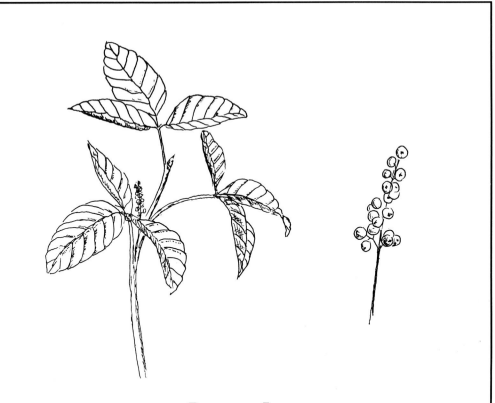

POISON IVY

It is important that everyone be able to recognize poison ivy, particularly children, who are more likely than adults to contact the plant in their short pathside explorations. Get to know the plant and its appearance in all seasons.

The most important identifying feature is the three leaves branching from a single stem. The leaves have smooth margins or a few coarse teeth around the edges. These leaves are green in the spring and summer, becoming red or dull yellow in the fall.

The plants are found in open woods, thickets and fence rows. Most poison ivy in Ontario grows to a height of 10 to 25 centimetres, but in some areas it appears as tall, woody climbing plants. Plants often grow in clumps and sometimes form large areas of ground cover along roadsides.

In May and June, flowers grow in small, branching clusters in the axils; the fruit is grey or whitish from August onward, and may persist throughout the winter.

All parts of the plant contain a volatile oil which can cause severe inflammation of the skin, with itching and blistering.

Avoid contact! If contact occurs, prompt washing with soap and water may remove the oil. It is possible to transfer the oil from exposed skin, footwear, clothing or the dog to other areas of skin. Children in particular should be cautioned in this regard.

Medical attention should be sought if the dermatitis is severe.

Drumlins in Otonabee Township, near the Indian River

1

ROCKS, DRUMLINS AND LAKES

Alan G. Brunger, Trent University

The complexity of physical features in Peterborough County may be simplified by thinking of a more or less equal division of its area into a southern glaciated lowland "half" and a northern Canadian Shield "half." The landscape and habitats of the two halves result from the different underlying geological structures: hard, older rocks in the north; younger, somewhat less resistant rocks, including clays, sands and gravels, in the south. The following section describes the geology, or underlying rocks, and the geomorphology, or surface landforms, of Peterborough County.

THE SOUTHERN HALF consists of two principal layers, the Pleistocene till and the Ordovician limestone. (Editor's note: Please do not give up just yet. Spend a few minutes with the illustration "Typical Geological Section in Southern Ontario." You will find it easy to understand these terms, and you will be able to be "one up" on your friends!)

The Pleistocene till or drift, is a relatively recent deposit (less than 1 million years) of a mixture of particles ranging in size from fine clay to large boulders. Occasionally the drift has been sorted by flowing water, and large deposits of particles of uniform size are found. Such locations may possess clay, sand, or gravel in such purity that they have been extracted for profit. These pits and quarries provide sites to view the pattern of glacial deposits.

A large ice sheet moving southwestward deposited various distinct depositional landforms: drumlins, end moraines, eskers, lake beds and erratics.

Drumlins are a notable feature in the Peterborough area owing to their frequent appearance and classic form. The county has one of the best drumlin fields in Canada. The drumlins are elongated in plan and asymmetrical in long profile, having a steeper glacier end (northeast locally) and a gentler trailing end (southwest locally). They rise as high as 60 metres and are believed to have been formed by immense pressure on drift under a flowing ice sheet. The best examples are in Otonabee Township, south of Keene on the shore of Rice Lake, and in the lake as islands. Easily accessible drumlins in Peterborough include Armour Hill and Trent University's Nassau campus.

The *end moraine* is a ridge of higher land with two local examples, the large Oak Ridges Moraine and the inconspicuous Dummer Moraine. The Oak Ridges Moraine rises to 100 metres locally and is believed to have been formed at the east-west junction of lobes of two separate ice sheets. The moraine was formed by the release of transported sediment as the lobes melted and is visible south of Rice Lake and in southern Cavan Township. The moraine was cleared for agriculture, but the sandy soils now support large-scale red pine reforestation.

The other end moraine of note is the Dummer Moraine, which crosses the county from WNW to ESE just south of the Kawartha Lakes. This moraine is an unimpressive feature which rises only a few metres as low hills. The Dummer Moraine is believed to have been formed during the recession of the last ice sheet, when a pause in the process permitted the accumulation of debris along the end of the melting ice for a relatively brief period of time. The Dummer Moraine is perhaps best viewed just north of the village of Warsaw, on the 1st Line of Dummer Township en route to the Warsaw Caves Conservation Area.

An *esker* is a serpentine ridge of sand and gravel rising to a maximum height of 25 metres and believed to have been deposited by meltwater streams flowing below retreating glaciers. Local eskers form distinct features west of Lakefield, north of Warsaw and near Norwood. They are useful both as sources of aggregate material and as well-drained natural routes such as the Sand Road west of Norwood and the Warsaw Road.

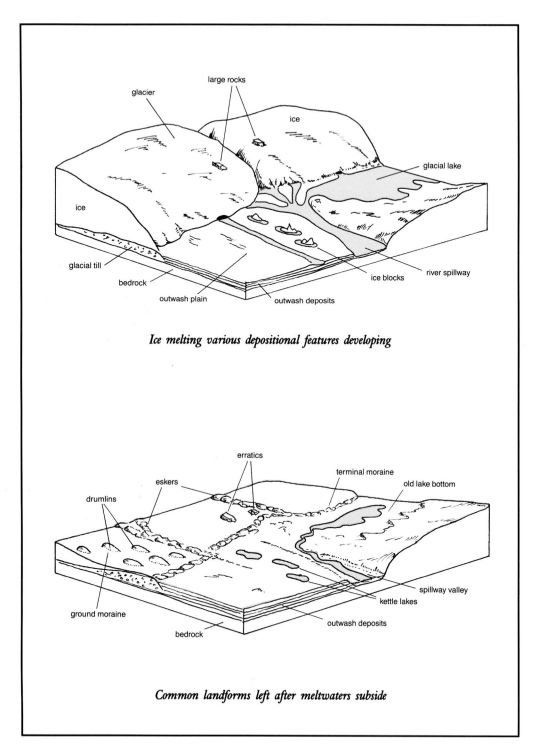

Ice melting various depositional features developing

Common landforms left after meltwaters subside

A typical geological section in southern Ontario

The *lake bed* of glacial Lake Peterborough was deposited in level layers of clay or sand southwest of the city near the present airport and may best be viewed from Highway 7 west of Brealey Drive or from Springville hill on Highway 28.

Another surface depositional feature derived from the ice sheets is the *erratic*, or isolated boulder, which lies unconformably on the rock below. Countless erratics occupy the county area. Most noteworthy is Council Rock at Buckhorn, which is believed to have been a focus for aboriginal peoples. Nearby are the Adam and Eve, or Kissing Rocks, a pair of granitic erratics.

A topographic relic from the Pleistocene era is the *spillway*, or channel, cut by massive rivers emerging from the stagnating ice sheet. The two principal spillways in Peterborough County are the valleys of the Otonabee and Indian rivers. The present rivers occupy barely a fraction of the capacity of the original spillways.

The Ordovician limestone strata form layers which have been buried by the younger glacial deposits. They are relatively resistant to erosion and result in some prominent landforms. The strata are most evident in the central part of the county, where they slope gently southwards and form cliffs, or scarps, on their northern edges in several locations.

These strata were deposited as level marine sediments in tropical seas 450 million years ago. They subsequently hardened and were uplifted and tilted to the south. Their character is predominantly calcareous limestone derived from ocean-dwelling organisms which have been fossilized. Notable layers include the Sherman Falls beds, which feature many brachiopods, and corals. These ...n the Lakefield area. ...wn as the Leray ...th relatively few ...s form the surface ...mmer Township ...own as *karst* is found, notably at the Warsaw Caves. The solubility of limestone is the reason for its relatively barren surface, as moisture rapidly percolates through solution cracks. Level, largely soil-less areas known as *alvars* support limited vegetation in the form of scattered bushes or trees with root systems capable of reaching the moister crevices.

More dramatic evidence of *karst* topography includes caves, canyons, open joints, disappearing streams, waterfalls and *kettles*. The latter are circular, bowl-like impressions in the limestone surface which have been formed by debris-laden streams as well as by solution. Numerous kettles exist at Warsaw Caves, ranging in diameter from a few centimetres to about 1 metre.

Over geological time, the Ordovician strata have been gradually eroded throughout northern Peterborough County and beyond. At the northern edge of the limestone, erosion has created a steep cliff, or scarp, which is some 30 metres high in places and best viewed in the southern shores of Lower Buckhorn and Lovesick lakes.

In the slow process of erosion, resistant portions of the strata remain isolated, as *outliers* or limestone "flats," some distance to the north of the main strata. They are surrounded by an expanse of older rocks in the Precambrian Shield. Some of these outliers are quite large, several square kilometres in size, forming distinct "islands" in the "sea" of older rocks, as near Flynn's Turn on Highway

Esker in Asphodel Township, near Norwood

36 in Harvey Township and near Woodview on 28 in Burleigh Township.

THE NORTHERN HALF of the county is part of the huge Precambrian Shield, a geological feature of great age and complexity which forms the surface of a large portion of Canada and which underlies much of the continent of North America. The resistant Shield rocks date from 600 to 1,200 million years and have diverse origins linked to the forces at work in the Earth's core.

Rock types include igneous, sedimentary and metamorphic forms. The igneous rocks were pushed up from the Earth's interior and subsequently cooled and hardened into a mass of crystals. On close inspection individual crystals may be detected with square, hexagonal, octagonal or polygonal form. Other parts of the Shield are sedimentary strata deposited on the beds of ancient

seas entirely devoid of life forms. Later on, these sedimentary and igneous rocks were subjected to intense heat and pressure during movements of the Earth's crust. Change, or metamorphosis, took place to create metamorphic rocks, which are commonly found in the northern part of Peterborough County. Such metamorphic rocks are often distinguishable by their rearranged crystalline form, such as massive white marble at Petroglyphs Provincial Park.

At Blue Mountain in Methuen Township, northeast of Stoney Lake, an igneous intrusion of nepheline syenite supports the only commercial mine of this material in Canada.

The Precambrian Shield was smoothed off by the grinding action of the massive ice sheet which removed much of the soil and loose surface debris and transported it to the south to form deposits such as the drumlins, moraines and erratics mentioned earlier. In

Little Lake, a glacial lake bed

places, the rocks bear surface grooves formed by the erosion of the advancing ice. Elsewhere, rounded knobs of rock are called "roches moutonnes," or sheeplike rocks, which became smooth on the northern, glacier, side and jagged on the southern side, where plucking of rock particles is believed to have occurred. One example is Lynch's Rock in Douro Township, also notable as an "inlier" of older hard Precambrian Shield projecting up through the surrounding younger Ordovician limestone. Another, smaller inlier is nearby at Galesburg on County Road 6. The most spectacular erratics are derived from the Precambrian Shield, such as those at Buckhorn.

LAKES AND RIVERS: The junction of the Ordovician and Precambrian rocks forms an irregular groove, or valley, in which lie several of the Kawartha Lakes. This valley formed as the relatively weaker limestones were eroded from the underlying Shield rocks. During the post-glacial period the valley became submerged and *glint,* or geological contact line, lakes — Bald, Lower Buckhorn, Lovesick and Stoney — formed along this significant junction, matching similar, much larger bodies of water elsewhere in Canada, such as Lake Huron, Winnipeg and Great Slave lakes.

Other Kawartha lakes — Balsam, Pigeon, Chemung, Clear and Rice — occupy pre-glacial valleys in the Ordovician strata, which became submerged after deglaciation, owing to drift deposits in their southern ends, toward which flowed pre-glacial streams. The whole drainage system was altered in the most recent historical period by damming of rivers for power supply and canal navigation, thus drowning more land and increasing the size of the lakes and adjacent wetland areas.

The numerous poorly drained bogs and marshes of the county occupy considerable areas and reflect the extent of impervious clay within the glacial deposits as well as the irregular topography which obstructs many of the streams. The latter have typically sluggish flow in spite of the elevation, some 200 metres above sea level. Many streams flow perversely north, exactly opposite to the regional drainage preference, which is towards Lake Ontario.

The wetlands that provide the most notable contrasts in landscape are found in the southern part of the county, notably the Cavan Bog, Miller Creek in Smith Township, and Buckley Lake in Douro. The best viewpoints for each are, respectively, from near Mount Pleasant on County Road 10, from lot 16 of the 7th Line of Smith, and from Highway 134 east of Lakefield. Numerous other smaller swamps occur in inter-drumlin *swales,* or valleys, or on lake margins.

SUMMARY: The pattern of geology and geomorphology in Peterborough County is relatively simple: older and harder rocks in the north, and younger and softer rocks in the south. As is evident from the foregoing, variations from this rule exist and affect the landscape locally in quite dramatic ways. The presence of deep soil and plentiful surface moisture dictates the precise habitat and surface species composition. The county thus possesses a wide variety of habitat as a consequence of infinite combinations of rock, soil, slope, moisture and geomorphology.

2

SILENT LAKE PROVINCIAL PARK

Ron Speck, Ministry of Natural Resources

Silent Lake Provincial Park offers a perfect environment for enjoying the natural beauty of the lower Canadian Shield. Close to the densely populated areas of southern Ontario yet secluded enough to be a peaceful haven, this Natural Environment Park is an ideal getaway spot. Its sparkling waters, rocky shoreline and green forests are typical of the "near north" of southern Ontario, and its fine camping and recreational facilities make it a popular place for outdoor pleasures.

Silent Lake Park contains 1,420 hectares of land and water off Highway 28, 25 kilometres north of Apsley (map ref. Q 16). Apart from the campground areas on the north shore of the lake, the park is undeveloped and in its natural state.

Logging brought settlement to the park area in the 1800s. The great white pines of the aboriginal forest were the targets of the early loggers, but cutting of both hardwoods and softwoods continued until well into this century. Forest fires also ravaged the land on more than one occasion during the logging era, so the trees in the park today are mostly second growth. Park visitors can see remains of the logging camps scattered throughout the area, as well as the huge, blackened stumps of trees that were long ago consumed by fire.

In the late 1800s a family called Patterson homesteaded at the head of the lake and tried, with little success, to make a living by farming the rocky, shallow soil. In 1927 a wealthy American built a lodge that attracted other American sportsmen, who came to fish and hunt in the unspoiled wilderness. Six Point Lodge operated for 40 years, until it was purchased by the Crown in 1967; in 1975 Silent Lake Provincial Park was officially opened.

Around Silent Lake the forest is a mixture of the deciduous and evergreen trees typical of this latitude. Birch, maple, hemlock, and white pine are the most common species. Of interest to amateur naturalists are the many varieties of wildflowers that grow throughout the park. Some unusual types, such as rose pogonia, rattlesnake fern and toothwort, may be discovered in the more isolated areas. Plants more commonly seen include several types of ferns and orchids, sedges and pitcher plants.

In 1985 a 145-hectare nature reserve zone was added to the east side of the park. The valleys of this area have 25 different fern species, including the narrow-leaved spleenwort, a fern which is rare in Ontario. A rare amphibian, the four-toed salamander, also occurs in this addition and is seldom encountered elsewhere in Ontario. This area is a

major asset to the park and is treated with special attention. To protect this area's significant features, no development will be allowed.

The park's mammals include otter, mink and beaver, which live in the marshy areas near the shoreline of the lake; deer can sometimes be spotted in the higher areas and are occasionally bold enough to venture quite close to the campgrounds.

Silent Lake lies in the transition zone between the southern deciduous forests and the northern coniferous forests; therefore it is home to both northern and southern species of plants and animals.

Birds that inhabit the park during the spring and summer months include the scarlet tanager and ruby-throated hummingbird, as well as more common species such as the bluejay, great blue heron, pileated woodpecker, chickadee and various types of warblers and thrushes. Ducks are common in the park during the migration season. The haunting cry of the loon can often be heard along the shoreline of Silent Lake.

Silent Lake can best be enjoyed by canoe; there are several rocky islands to explore and, from the water, there is no evidence of human habitation. Three interconnecting lakes provide interesting trips for those who wish to paddle further from the campgrounds. There are three launching areas in the

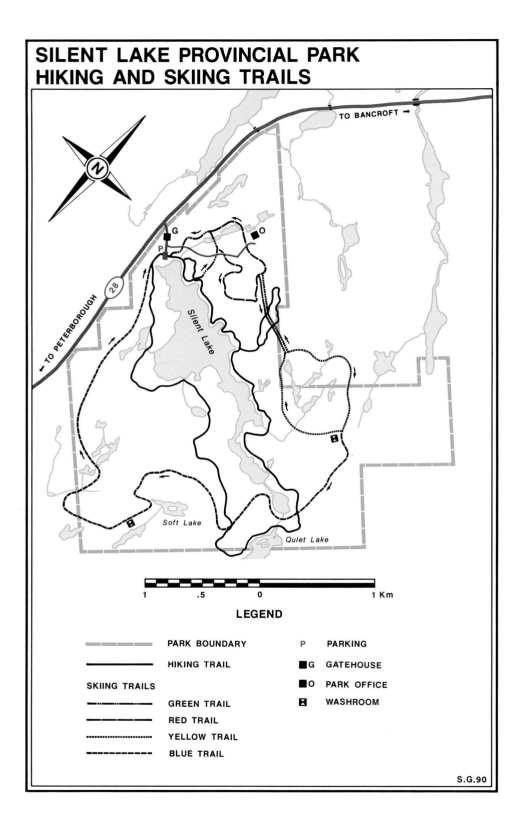

SILENT LAKE PROVINCIAL PARK HIKING AND SKIING TRAILS

TO BANCROFT →

TO PETERBOROUGH

28

Silent Lake

Soft Lake

Quiet Lake

1   .5   0   1 Km

LEGEND

———————	PARK BOUNDARY
———————	HIKING TRAIL

SKIING TRAILS

—··—··—··—	GREEN TRAIL
————————	RED TRAIL
··················	YELLOW TRAIL
— — — — —	BLUE TRAIL

P	PARKING
■G	GATEHOUSE
■O	PARK OFFICE
⊠	WASHROOM

S.G.90

park, two near the campgrounds and one in the day-use area, and canoes are available for rent. To preserve the peace of the natural environment, no motorboats are allowed in the park.

Whether you are an ardent hiker, a nature lover or a family out for a stroll, you will find a trail at Silent Lake just for you. The park's three well-marked hiking trails offer visitors the opportunity to explore the natural environment on foot.

The lakehead loop, a 1.5-kilometre trail can be walked in approximately 30 minutes. It starts at the bridge crossing Silent Creek, just east of the open area at the head of the lake. From there it follows the lakeshore among cedar and black ash to a point overlooking Peaches Island, which affords a view right down Silent Lake to the narrows. After a climb to higher ground through stands of red oak and maple, the trail makes a steep descent and eventually returns to the bridge where it started.

Bonnie's Pond trail, a 3-kilometre interpretive trail, starts at the Pincer Bay parking lot and winds its way through many interesting and unique features in the eastern portion of the park. At a leisurely pace it will take you about 1 1/4 hours to walk this trail. Shortly after the start of the trail, there is a stand of mature beech trees. If you look carefully at the bark of these trees, you will probably find the claw marks of bears that have climbed the tree to reach beech nuts in the fall. Also along this trail you will find beaver ponds and the blackened stumps of huge pines burnt in extensive forest fires in the 1800s.

The lakeshore trail is 15 kilometres in length and is for seasoned hikers. Rugged hills, beaver meadows, hardwood forest, cedar and black ash swamps, and spectacular lookout points are some of the delights of this hiking trail. Canoeists can join the trail from various points around the shoreline, but overnight camping is allowed at designated sites only.

When the snow falls, Silent Lake Provincial Park offers a totally different kind of outdoor experience. More than 40 kilometres of cross-country ski trails are groomed and track-set each winter; different parts of the trail system are designed for novice, intermediate and skilled skiers. Ski lessons and rental equipment are available, and the trails are patrolled by members of the Canadian Ski Patrol Association. There are three warm-up huts along the trails, and a primitive camping area with basic facilities (firewood and vault toilets) can be reached by skiing or walking.

Bald eagle

Silent Lake

Marsh edge

3

HIKING TRAILS IN PETROGLYPHS PROVINCIAL PARK

Lisa Roach

Petroglyphs Provincial Park is located 56 kilometres northeast of Peterborough, Ontario (map ref. P 16). From Peterborough, take Highway 28 north to Woodview. On the outskirts of Woodview, turn right onto Northey's Bay Road and travel approximately 11 kilometres. A large sign indicates the park entrance.

The park is situated on the southern fringe of the Canadian Shield, in a region with numerous lakes, streams and wetlands alternating with low hills, ridges of bare rock, and stretches of unbroken conifer and deciduous forests.

The park has several trails to accommodate people who enjoy either short or long hikes. All trails are well-worn footpaths and are well signed; it is not advisable to wander from the paths, as even experienced hikers have become lost in the forest! Walking shoes or hiking boots with non-slip soles are essential.

The park brochure has a map of the trails, and there is another brochure for the Nanabush trail. These are available at the entrance office or at the petroglyph site during the summer season.

The three principal trails start from the main parking lot area. A billboard by the washrooms displays the trail map and shows the Marsh trail exiting separately and the High Falls and Nanabush trails sharing their first 1.4 kilometres.

At the beginning of the Nanabush trail are exposed areas of limestone with raised ridges of pink granite. These ridges are called dykes and were formed when the soft bedrock weathered over the years, leaving the harder rock protruding above the surface.

There are 11 small stone cairns along the interpretive Nanabush trail, and the abstract symbols on these cairns are described in the folder.

In the spring and early summer, many wildflowers carpet the trail, with fringed polygala or gaywings being especially evident.

One large and several smaller wetlands have been created by beaver dams. Great blue heron are common, and ducks, Canada geese, water snakes and turtles may be seen in the first large swamp. If walking quietly, deer may be observed browsing. The trees here are elm, black ash and white cedar. The many dead trees seen in the wetlands were killed by the raised water level.

High Falls

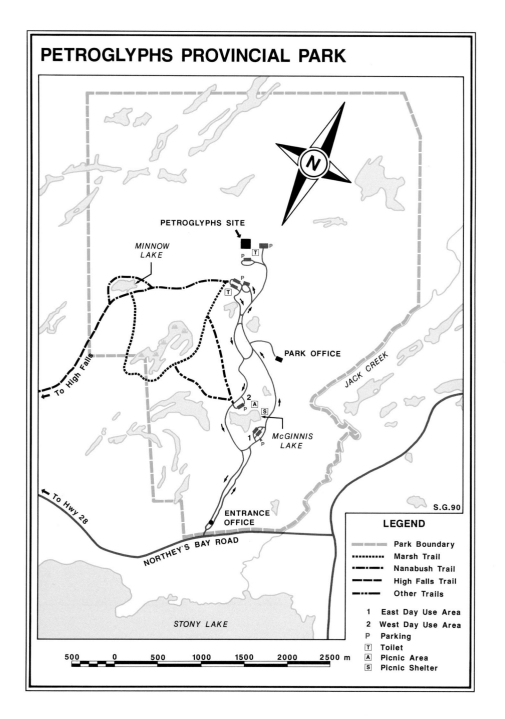

PETROGLYPHS PROVINCIAL PARK

PETROGLYPHS SITE

MINNOW LAKE

PARK OFFICE

JACK CREEK

To High Falls

2 West Day Use Area

McGINNIS LAKE

1 East Day Use Area

To Hwy 28

S.G.90

ENTRANCE OFFICE

NORTHEY'S BAY ROAD

STONY LAKE

LEGEND

- Park Boundary
- Marsh Trail
- Nanabush Trail
- High Falls Trail
- Other Trails

1 East Day Use Area
2 West Day Use Area
P Parking
T Toilet
A Picnic Area
S Picnic Shelter

500   0   500   1000   1500   2000   2500 m

Between 1871 and 1911 the park and surrounding area suffered a period of intensive lumbering and forest fires; extensive reforestation is evident, more so on the Marsh trail.

At the southwest corner of Minnow Lake the trails diverge. The Nanabush trail continues to be marked with yellow blazes on trees, and loops around the north shore of the small lake. The steepest hill is near the start of this segment, leading to high ground along the north shore, with fine views of the lake and surrounding forest. Largely because of this hill, one would class the walk as moderately difficult. At the east end of the lake, one joins the entry trail to return to the parking area, having walked 3 kilometres in 1 1/2 hours or more.

The High Falls trail continues west from the junction and is marked with blue and white hiking symbols. The falls are 3.6 kilometres further on; the round trip requiring at least 4 hours to complete.

Shortly past the junction, the landscape changes, with shallower soil and more outcroppings of bedrock. There are more open areas with grasses, ferns and lichens. Further along the trail is another boardwalk and two log bridges, which provide excellent wildlife viewing.

Three-quarters of the way along this trail, hikers leave the park boundary and enter the Peterborough Crown Game Preserve, established in 1927 as a refuge for white-tailed deer and other game animals. Black bear, moose, and timber and brush wolves are known to inhabit the preserve and the park. Five-lined skinks (small lizards) may sometimes be seen on outcroppings of rock or emerging from crevices.

On higher ground, there are large stands of red and white pine, with smaller areas of spruce and mixed hardwood such as white birch, sugar maple and red oak.

On the south shore of Minnow Lake, hikers can see the remains of a cabin which once housed loggers; the cabin's design and the small size of the logs suggest it was built in the early 1900s.

Ruffed grouse, downy, hairy and pileated woodpeckers, heron, hawks and warblers may be seen in temperate months, while blue and grey jays reside year-round, and bald and golden eagles may be seen in the winter months.

The falls are on Eels Creek, as it descends to Stoney Lake, and they are very picturesque and provide a pleasant spot for lunch. (Author's note: Be careful. We watched a dog go over the falls, and a child camper go fortunately only part way before a daring rescue.) Hikers with local knowledge may follow the creek south to the Northey's Bay Road; otherwise, one should follow the trail back to the main parking lot.

The third trail, the Marsh trail, goes south around a marsh and returns north to join the first common trail near the east side of Minnow Lake. It is densely forested, mainly with pine, and is sufficiently hilly to be classed as moderately difficult. The trail is well travelled and carpeted with pine needles; a very pleasant 2-hour walk.

Finally, there are two additional shorter trails which start at the West Day Use Area and join the Marsh trail for portions of their course. One trail is ridged and rocky, the other passes wetlands. The wooden bridge crosses an ancient stream bed made by glacial meltwater.

If one has not seen the petroglyphs previously, a visit to the glyph site provides an interesting conclusion to the day.

McGinnis Lake

4

KE-NO-MAH-GAY-WAH-KON

The Teaching Rock

Lorenzo Whetung, Curve Lake

Petroglyphs

Amid the rugged granite rocks and tall pines that extend to the north of Stoney Lake near Peterborough lies a fine display of rock carvings. The site where these pictures are located is called the Peterborough Petroglyphs. The word petroglyph means rock (petro) carving (glyph). There are about 1,000 pictographs (pictures used as signs or symbols) at the site, making it one of the largest such sites in North America. Tens of thousands of people from around the world visit the Peterborough Petroglyphs from May to October each year.

The petroglyphs are located in one of Ontario's most scenic wilderness parks. The park has an abundance of wildlife and wildflowers in a variety of natural habitats. In this area, granite and gneiss rocks predominate, but amid the bold red and grey masses of granite there is a rare outcropping of white crystalline limestone. It is in this sparkling white rock that early native people chose to make their etchings.

Native people, or *Anishnabe* as they refer to themselves, have their own understanding and interpretation of the Peterborough Petroglyphs. Their appreciation of these pictographs has been handed down from generation to generation. The *Anishnabe* refer to the pictures in the rock as *Ke-no-mah-gay-wah-kon*, which means "the rocks that teach." In this capacity the rocks still function among the traditional societies of the *Anishnabe* people and provide them with a special perspective which gives the rocks life and meaning. The *Anishnabe* people regard the site as a sacred location and hold it in great reverence.

The pictures hold many meanings and provide many teachings. The creators of these pictographs drew natural subjects with smooth flowing lines and sometimes incorporated the characteristics of the rock, its cracks and fissures, into their work to enhance their messages.

The carvings raise many questions. What messages and implications are there in the female figure that is split by a natural occurrence of red granite? Why does the large turtle figure appear to be laying its eggs? Why are there so many turtles on the rock? When were these pictures carved? Do the human figures represent individuals? What happened to the people who were responsible for the creation of this magnificent collection of rock carvings? The answers to some of these questions may be found within the oral traditions of the *Anishnabe* people.

The *Anishnabe* people speak of their migration from the East Coast, and of this rock marking their arrival. They also speak of powerful medicine people with healing abilities and the gift of vision, both present and future, which is said to be a gift of the red man. The carvings on the rock are testimony to those early times and to the special powers of the *Anishnabe*. Those who sought knowledge and enlightment would come to the rock to seek its strength and power, and to be tutored and have the stories of the rock

explained to them. Even today, the elders of various native groups tell of being taken to the rock by their grandparents when they were children.

There are many theories and speculations about the pictographs on the rock. Many people who visit the rock experience powerful emotions and leave with new understanding. Others who seek to better understand the messages intended by the carvers must seek out the elders who listened to explanations passed on to them in their own childhood. It is important, when trying to understand the pictures, to view

them in the context of their creators and not allow present-day perceptions to intrude.

The rock pictures are a living legacy created by the native people of Canada to be shared by all mankind. *Ke-no-mab-gay-wab-kon* (the rocks that teach) is home to the white-tailed deer, the pileated woodpecker, ravens, eagles, groundhogs, snakes, and beavers, as well as the people who visit. Together we live and learn as one family. Treat this site as sacred and listen for the messages it has to tell.

Meegwetch (thank you).

Petroglyphs

White-tailed deer

Boreal owl

Cross-country skiers

PETERBOROUGH CROWN GAME PRESERVE

Gordon Berry

The Peterborough Crown Game Preserve covers some 221 square kilometres located on the west side of Highway 28 between Haultain and Apsley (map ref. P 16). Most of the area is Crown land, with the exception of some patented lands around the perimeter and around Jack Lake.

In the early 1920s many animal preserves were established in Ontario on the theory that animals in the protected zones would multiply and provide a continuous supply of game to the surrounding areas. Over the years it became obvious that wildlife resources could not be stockpiled in this manner without producing severe stress on the range and populations within the preserves. As a result, many preserves were abolished.

The Peterborough Preserve has always been an important wintering area for deer. In late fall, deer move into the preserve to take advantage of the good coniferous cover, which provides them with protection against the deep snow and the cold. There is also a resident herd that lives there all the year round. The latter show little fear of man and are often seen by visitors. The total deer population is high and has resulted in some heavy browsing, which has affected the regeneration of young trees and shrubs.

Deer are poorly adapted for survival in snow. Their small hoofs penetrate deeply, and when snow depth exceeds 50 centimetres, the deer have difficulty moving between cover and food. There is evidence that in years of heavy snowfall some deer in the area starve.

The preserve's gently rolling terrain has numerous rock ridges covered by a mixture of conifers and hardwoods. The uplands are characterized by pines, hemlock, white spruce, white birch, sugar maple and red oak. In the lower depressions, where there is more moisture retention, cedar, balsam, tamarack and black spruce are found. Many areas have a rather parklike appearance, a result of heavy grazing and the naturally sparse undergrowth in upland sites, which have shallow soils and are overshaded by mature trees.

Beaver are active in some parts of the preserve. In times of expanding population, their activities have drowned out some cedar browse and contributed to the depletion of food for the deer.

Whenever deer are present, timber wolves, their natural predators, are also to be found. There are several packs in the preserve, and while these animals are rarely seen by visitors, a keen observer can find evidence of their presence in the remains of deer kills, tracks, scats and fur pellets.

Often when forest and park lands are used for more than one purpose, there is some conflict of interests, and frequently neither purpose is well served. This is not the case with the Peterborough Crown Game Preserve. Excellent compatible land use is made of this area for the protection of game and the enjoyment of cross-country skiers.

The Ministry of Natural Resources issued the Kawartha Nordic Ski Club a land-use permit to develop some 60 kilometres of wilderness cross-country ski trails. The trails are on Crown lands adjacent to Eels Creek and Highway 28, between Apsley and Haultain. Extensive, cleared and well-marked trails lace the woods and provide some of the best cross-country skiing in Ontario. There are three access points: one at Haultain beneath the bridge over Eels Creek; another at the Simmond's parking lot on the east side of Highway 28 a short distance north of Haultain; and a third entrance off McFadden Road just beyond the fairgrounds in Apsley, near the Whispering Pines Senior Citizens Home.

Two long trails, 2 to 3 kilometres apart, run north and south, roughly parallel with Eels Creek and the highway. These two trails extend for about 16 kilometres before combining into a single track for a further 2

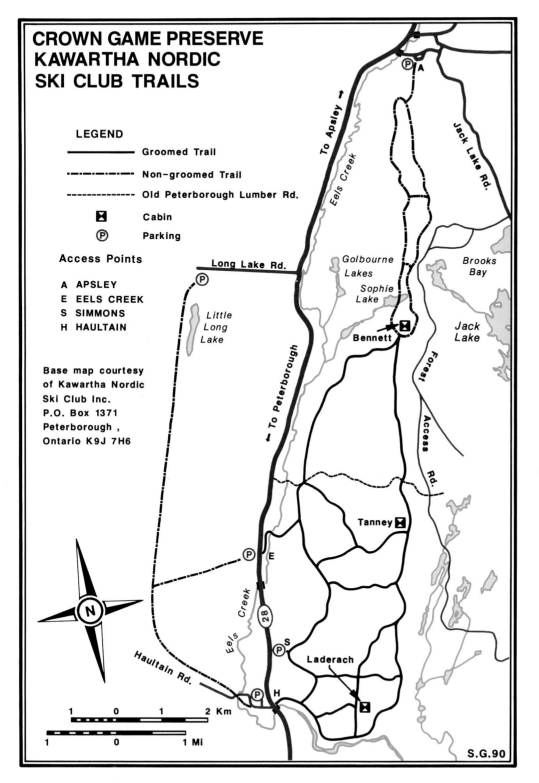

CROWN GAME PRESERVE KAWARTHA NORDIC SKI CLUB TRAILS

LEGEND

———————— Groomed Trail

—·—·—·—·— Non-groomed Trail

------------ Old Peterborough Lumber Rd.

☒ Cabin

Ⓟ Parking

Access Points

A APSLEY
E EELS CREEK
S SIMMONS
H HAULTAIN

Base map courtesy
of Kawartha Nordic
Ski Club Inc.
P.O. Box 1371
Peterborough ,
Ontario K9J 7H6

N

1 0 1 2 Km

1 0 1 Mi

S.G.90

kilometres to Apsley. There are numerous connecting paths between the parallel trails, which enable users to select a loop of almost any length. The southern end of the trail system is particularly well developed, with shorter and easier trail loops. The northern sections offer longer and more challenging trails.

There are three cabins at strategic locations along the trails. These cabins are intended as warm-up shelters and for emergencies. They are not to be used for overnight stays!

The trails are groomed regularly and maps displayed at every trail junction show route alternatives with directions and distance between points. The Kawartha Nordic Ski Club, a non-profit organization, has developed these excellent trails and is worthy of support.

While these trails have been developed and are maintained for cross-country skiing, they may also be used for summer hiking.

A word of caution. This is a wilderness area, these trails are not patrolled or in frequent use, except during the cross-country ski season. Persons using the trails do so at their own risk and should always let someone know where they are going before leaving home.

EELS CREEK BY CANOE

Gordon Berry

The Eels Creek route to Stoney Lake provides an undisturbed wilderness experience within a 40-minute drive of the city of Peterborough. There is not a single cottage or piece of developed land between Haultain and the bridge near the river mouth at Stoney Lake. The trip covers a distance of about 10 kilometres and is well within the abilities of any modest canoer. The route is conveniently divided into three sections by the need to stop at Ludgate Falls and High Falls. Both falls require the canoe to be portaged. The first is a short lift-over of about 50 metres. A longer, but not difficult, portage is required at High Falls.

Start the Eels Creek run at Haultain, on Highway 28 about 1.5 kilometres north of Woodview, (map ref. P 16). Turn left immediately after crossing the Haultain bridge. You will find an open space at the end of the short lane where you may safely leave your car. Mr. Don Church generously allows parking on his property and access to the water from his land for a small charge; see the small box on the garage wall. You will need to place a second car at the bridge over Eels Creek on the Northey's Bay Road, where the trip ends.

From below, the bridge at Haultain is something of a surprise. It is an old wooden trestle bridge, disguised from above with asphalt paving, and boasts several rows of wooden support piles rising from a shallow, sandy river bottom. At first the river twists and turns invitingly among large willows that form a shady vault above the water. The banks are lush with royal and ostrich ferns, and there are many signs of raccoon and beaver activity in the soft mud along the shore. About 0.5 kilometres downstream the river widens, and here herons and wading birds feed in the shallows. In late summer, the occasional purple-fringed orchis may be spotted on the north bank or a few small stands of cardinal flower may be found along the moist margins of the river. The spiky blue flowers of pickerel weed are common along this route, but just before the first small rapids is a bed of white-flowered pickerel weed, which is a much less common variety.

An excellent supply of food and water plants make this area a favourite breeding ground for several species of waterfowl, and the excited splashes of a mother duck and her brood skittering towards the shelter of the bankside reeds is a common sight.

Eels Creek

Water lily

The first rapids are formed by a small drop in the water level between two flat rocks. There is a signed portage path on the left bank, about 15 metres long. The more proficient canoer may wish to run these rapids on the right-hand side of the channel.

Some good campsites have been established by the Ministry of Natural Resources along Eels Creek. These are usually located in attractive areas where there is good, deep water for swimming. The sites are well marked with the familiar yellow signs nailed to shoreline trees.

In the next few kilometres there are a few swifts, stretches where the water runs a little faster and dimples the surface or ruffles with short lines and vees of lacy foam. These swifts are quite small and should not discourage even novice paddlers.

The sound of falling water will alert the traveller to the yellow portage marker as the canoe approaches Ludgate Falls. The sign is on the right-hand side of the river, where there is a good landing spot and an easy path around the wide, rocky falls. This is a great place for a rest and some refreshment,

or a swim in the wide pool below the falls. Beware of poison ivy, both here and at High Falls, where there are usually a few patches to catch the unwary.

The second section of river, from Ludgate Falls to High Falls, is a comfortable paddle, with time to enjoy some very pleasant scenery. Deer are plentiful in this area, as it adjoins the Peterborough Crown Game Reserve. Sometimes, when the canoe approach is very quiet, deer can be seen drinking at the water's edge.

High Falls is the major attraction along this route. The falls are a beautiful sight as the water tumbles some 10 metres over rounded granite boulders into the stream below. A hiking trail from the Petroglyphs Provincial Park ends here, and a few fishermen, who have come upstream from Stoney Lake, are often to be found below the falls.

The falls are hidden when approached from above. The river splits into two narrow channels, with the main current of water moving to the left, behind an outcrop of rock. Another small tributary branches to the right between the trees. The canoeist can first land on the right bank and explore a spectacular curving rock cut, overhung by trees, where the water splashes into a small shady pool. In summer, this rock basin provides an excellent whirlpool bath for the more venturesome. The pool should not be approached in spring run-off or when water levels are high. The main flow cascades over open rocks and is best viewed from above on the left bank. There are excellent picnic sites on the flat rocks above the falls or on the right bank below the falls.

Portage the canoe around High Falls on the left bank. There is a yellow marker in a tree as you come close to shore, and there are painted arrows on the flat rocks of the portage path to guide you to the river below. After re-launching the canoe you will discover that the river opens immediately into Second Lake. An excellent campsite is to be found on the shore of this lake, sheltered from the wind and offering good swimming and fishing possibilities. (Note: Hang all food packs high overnight to avoid raccoon damage!)

The river leaves this lake on the south side, so it is best to keep near the right bank. A narrow, but easily negotiated, channel runs down from the lake into a broad stretch of water with some delightful scenery. This is another point where deer are often seen; otter have also been seen playing in this location. After a kilometre or so, the river widens into First Lake and you should keep to the left-hand shore. A break in the tree line indicates the opening on the other side of the lake where a short stretch of river runs down into Stoney Lake.

There is a good place to take out the canoe just before reaching the Northey's Bay Road bridge. Below the bridge is a short, sharp rocky cut, known locally as Suicide Rapids, which are not negotiable with a canoe.

THE KAWARTHA LAKES

Enid Mallory

According to the *Trent Canal Guide* published in 1911, there are 76,317 hectares of water which drain into and flow down the Otonabee and Trent rivers to Lake Ontario. Along the way these waters form a chain of lakes we call the Kawarthas. These lakes, and the streams that run into and out of them, have shaped the lives of the people who live here.

Northern Kawartha lakes lie on the hard crystalline rock of the Canadian Shield, but where southern lakes lie, the granite is overlain by limestone and glacial till. This difference gives us two kinds of Kawartha lakes: the deeper northern lakes whose rugged shores grow white and red pine and white spruce; and the shallow southern lakes whose shorelines favour sugar maple and beech, now mostly cleared for agriculture or urban homes.

For the new arrival — a Mississauga Indian in the late 1700s or an Irish immigrant in the 1800s — the lakes and rivers provided transportation, contact by water or ice with neighbouring settlers, and a way to move goods and produce when roads were non-existent or almost impassable.

The idea of a canal system to link lakes and by-pass rapids, with locks and dams to control water flow, was conceived early. The idea probably occurred to every person who hefted a heavy load around rapids or got stuck in a shallow. Champlain, moving along with his Huron warriors, may have given it some thought. Certainly the first settlers did.

The canal was not built overnight. From the first lock at Bobcaygeon in 1833, it was a dream the pioneers passed on to their sons and daughters until the waterway was completed in 1920. The first improvements were designed to meet the needs of lumber barons moving logs. For almost a century lumbering was the main force in Kawartha life. It provided hard cash, excitement and pride for the strong, tough men waging war on the great forest. As in all wars, its army robbed and plundered and left great areas bereft. On granite rock, shorelines denuded of trees soon lost their thin layers of topsoil to erosion.

Settlers whose land lay in the southern Kawartha region found a rich and

Loon family

Kawartha Lakes

kindly land beneath the forest. But those who built their barns on granite or on the Dummer Moraine, along the edge of the Shield, found the going hard indeed.

An alternative to farming presented itself as tourists appeared on Rice Lake and began moving north. These adventurers began to affect the Kawartha Lakes as early as the 1870s. They inspired local people to develop a tourist economy based on lakes which would remain pristine and wild — or so it seemed at the time. They came to hunt and fish and to stay at lodges and hotels built by enterprising settlers. In time, many of them turned into cottagers: they wanted longer than a week at a lodge; they wanted to own an island on Stoney Lake or a piece of shoreline on Sturgeon. Their love of the Kawarthas protected it on the one hand and exploited it on the other.

The lake region got its name in 1907, when the Bobcaygeon village council was looking for an advertising slogan. The council went to the Curve Lake Indians for help, and Martha Whetung suggested "Kawatha," which meant "bright waters and happy lands." By the time the Kawartha Lakes Association was formed in 1900, an "r" had been added to the spelling.

Each lake has its own aura arising from its geology, its scenery and the people who have lived on its shores. Rice, Katchewanooka, Clear, Stoney, Buckhorn, Pigeon, Sturgeon, Cameron and Scugog are the big lakes, but Lovesick and Lower Buckhorn, attached to Buckhorn, and Big Bald and Little Bald, attached to Pigeon are sometimes considered separate lakes. Other lakes, like Sandy, Big Cedar, Catchacoma, Mississauga, Anstruther and Four

Mile Lake are considered part of the Kawartha region.

Since the lumber trade declined, use of the lakes has been mainly recreational. Emphasis on fishing or hunting, canoeing or sailing, camping or cottage-building varied from one lake to another and changed from one decade to another.

In the earliest years people came to campsite or cottage by canoe, but by the late 19th century they could reach Lakefield or Lindsay by train, then travel by steamboat to their destination. Now we come by car.

At the cottage or resort hotel in 1912 we might have formed a picnic party to Eels Creek by canoe or attended a regatta with canoe races, gunnel bobbing and sailboat competitions, or we might have gone on a moonlight steamboat excursion.

At the cottage in 1990 we may still take a canoe trip to Eels Creek, but we are also likely to roar around in power boats or on water skis behind them. Our grandparents' mahogany runabouts and cedar-strip canoes are rare collector items now; windsurfers and jet-skis are the new toys.

The early camper would have pitched his tent almost anywhere on a wilderness shoreline. Campers in the southern Kawarthas are now limited to provincial parks on Rice, Stoney and Balsam lakes, to public or private campgrounds, or to sites available to boaters on Trent Canal land at the locks. In the northern Kawarthas it is still possible to camp in the wilderness on Crown-land canoe routes.

People living in the Kawarthas fight a new fight now, quite different from the lumbermen's war on the forest. We struggle to keep the bright waters and

Burleigh Falls

happy lands which Martha Whetung described with the word "Kawatha," and to protect them from overuse and drastic change.

There are real fears that overuse is changing the lakes in ways that may be tragic and irreversible. Cottage associations are conducting lake-capacity studies in an attempt to plan for the future and find ways to protect the waters.

Education and understanding can help; people who treat their lawns with fertilizer and herbicides, which leach into the lakes, need to know that they are killing the water they love. A new concept of wild beauty can replace the manicured-lawn syndrome. Families from Toronto need to arrive here in one car instead of three. And could we reverse the trend toward higher horsepower? After all, the quintessential Kawartha craft is not a motorboat, it's a canoe!

These 76,317 hectares of moving water have shaped a beautiful lake district, which has been improved by the people who joined the lakes to make a continuous waterway from Lake Ontario to Georgian Bay. Can we continue to improve the Kawarthas or will we destroy them by overuse? Whether we use these lakes wisely or squander them foolishly, their waters and shorelines will continue to shape our lives.

SELWYN CONSERVATION AREA

Kathy Reid, Otonabee Region Conservation Authority

The sand beach, picnic areas, open fields, and hiking trails of the Selwyn Conservation Area provide visitors with many hours of relaxation and outdoor recreation.

The Selwyn Conservation Area is located on the northeast shore of Chemong Lake, 27 kilometres from the city of Peterborough (map ref. O 17).

The 29-hectare parcel of land was acquired by the Otonabee Region Conservation Authority in 1973. It provides a multi-purpose day-use facility with access to Chemong Lake, while protecting the natural features of the property. It boasts a variety of habitat, ranging from marginal wetland to woodland to open field. Many wildflowers, including closed (or bottle) gentian, members of the violet family, and spotted jewelweed can be found, and white-tailed deer, skunk, raccoon, meadow vole and field mouse are a few of the animals that inhabit the area. The great blue heron is a frequent visitor, feeding in the wetlands and along the shoreline. Visitors will often see songbirds, as well as the fish-eaters, including the belted kingfisher and the osprey.

Excellent swimming facilities are provided by the gently sloping sand beach. Change houses and vault toilets are provided. Picnickers may enjoy the secluded barbecues and tables or the convenience of the picnic shelter, all within close walking distance of the beach. Large playing fields are ideal for group activities. Organized groups may also use the field area for overnight camping by arrangement.

Recreational boating enthusiasts will appreciate the boat launching and docking facilities provided at Selwyn. From here, boaters can cruise the Kawartha Lakes and access the Trent-Severn Waterway. Overnight docking can also be arranged.

The hiking trail begins from the beach area. It is 3.5 kilometres in length and takes on average 40 minutes to complete. As you follow the trail you will hike through areas of thick cedar woods, a stand of sugar maple and American beech, and open fields. Approximately half the length of the trail follows the shoreline of Chemong Lake. If you are fortunate you may catch a glimpse of wood ducks which nest in a wooden nesting box on shore. You may also find signs of white-tailed deer, pileated woodpecker and yellow-bellied sapsucker. Cross-country skiers enjoy the trail throughout the winter months.

An additional and enjoyable 2-to-3-kilometre walk can be added to the hiking trails of Selwyn. To the right of the Selwyn Conservation Area entrance gate is an abandoned road, which runs for about a kilometre along the south side of the property. The old road runs in a relatively straight line until it meets the 13th Line of Smith Township. Along the trail are many wild fruit trees which are scattered about the old split-rail fences. There is a good example of a snake fence on the left-hand side of the trail, a form of fencing that is fast disappearing in Ontario. It is interesting to speculate that these trees probably grew from apples eaten by field workers who tossed their cores into the bushes many decades ago. The laborious clearing of the land involved not only the felling of trees and removal of their stubborn roots, but also the endless collection of rocks from the poor soil. The rocks were dragged on horse-drawn stone boats to the sides of the fields, where they formed fences to keep in cattle. Great piles of these stones can also be seen in various places on the conservation property. There is also an abundance of wild grapes in this area, many vines climbing as much as 20 metres into the trees and trailing in long strands to the ground.

When you reach the road junction, turn left and follow a gravelled cottage service road signed to Selwyn Bay. Follow this road almost to its end. At first the road passes by abandoned

Selwyn shoreline

pastures covered with bushes and small trees. Eventually cottages appear on the right-hand side and glimpses of the lake can be seen through the trees and between the cottages. Watch for a maple woodlot on your left. This fine stand of trees is on the Selwyn Conservation Area property and covers the point of land which looks across to the Curve Lake Indian Reserve. There is a small footpath leading into the woods, and after crossing the fence line, it branches to the left and to the right. Both trails will lead you back to the beach area within the park. The trail to the left will pass through bush and open fields and is relatively flat. The trail to the right takes you through the woods and, by a circuitous route, to the lakeshore and tunnels of arching cedars leading to the beach and main activity areas of the park.

Trout lily

THE HEBER ROGERS WILDLIFE AREA

Gordon Berry

The Heber Rogers Wildlife Area is a small parcel of land donated to the Otonabee Region Conservation Authority by Mrs. R. Rogers in memory of her husband, the son of R.B. Rogers, who designed the Peterborough lift locks. The property is reached from the Kawartha Park Road off Highway 28, just south of Burleigh Falls (map ref. 0 16). There is a sign on the right-hand side of the road about 0.5 kilometres in from the highway, with a small parking lot just off the road.

This woodlot is chiefly of interest as a place to see spring wildflowers. A little-used winding path, marked with yellow markers nailed to trees, runs through the woods for nearly a kilometre. The trail emerges at the back of the parking lot belonging to Kawartha Park Marina on Clear Lake, and there is a large conservation area sign here also.

The land is situated on a limestone table so thinly covered with topsoil that the limestone rock is totally exposed in many places. The mature trees have been cut, but there is a good variety of new-growth ash, ironwood, oak, poplar and maple. Wild roses, wild raspberries and wild strawberries abound, often growing from cracks in the limestone.

The lightly shaded floor of the wood makes it ideal for wildflowers. In spring, the woods present a display of violets, trilliums, hepatica, spring beauty, Dutchman's breeches, lady's-slipper, squirrel corn and wild leek, among many others.

Early in the season, the marshy area is only passable with rubber boots, but it holds a variety of common flowering plants and ferns that enjoy a damp environment.

Hepatica

Great blue heron

THE INDIAN RIVER BY CANOE

Gordon Berry

Anyone viewing the gentle stream that flows from Stoney Lake to Rice Lake would have difficulty imagining these placid waters as a roaring torrent. Yet during the last ice age this stream is believed to have carried volumes of water comparable to the St. Lawrence River. As the ice cap retreated, the meltwaters flowed out to the sea along this general route. Evidence of this earlier river valley can be seen in the wide trench in which Lang Village rests and in the deep chasm at Warsaw.

While the entire length of this river is only canoeable in the early spring, there are some small sections which are deep enough to provide reasonable paddle depth for summer trips. These short sections offer delightful moments of tranquil beauty close to the city of Peterborough.

Warsaw Village to the Warsaw Gorge

At the north end of the village of Warsaw and close beside the United Church, one branch of the Indian River nudges against the road and provides good public access to the water. The river here is wide and shallow, forming a small lake above the control dam.

Once on the water, head north against the gentle current. A short paddle along a shallow but easily navigated channel among some flooded tree stumps brings the visitor to the junction with the main river, which skirts around the town. Good canoeing depth is then available all the way to the Warsaw Caves Conservation Area property.

At first there are some homes and cottages along the shore, but these gradually disappear as the banks become steeper and access to the water becomes more difficult. The transition from a broad river valley at Warsaw Village to the 65-metre-deep gorge at Warsaw Caves provides an interesting variety of habitat over a very short distance. Close to Warsaw, beds of reeds and rushes resound with the harsh calls of redwing blackbirds and kingbirds.

Often the approach of a canoe will disturb a great blue heron patiently fishing for frogs or fish in the shallows. These large, alert and wary birds take to the air in stately, leisurely flight,

Indian River from lookout

Indian River

usually to land only a short distance upstream, to be sighted again and again each time the canoe approaches. Great blue herons nest in colonies in the tops of trees and may fly considerable distances each day to their feeding territories.

As the banks become steeper, chickadees converse among shady cedars, kingfishers flash above the water and the patient and observant paddler may chance upon beaver, muskrat and mink.

The gorge has a special charm. Viewed from above, its width and depth are commanding, even majestic, but from the water it offers a more personal perspective. The visitor experiences the peaceful serenity of the landscape. However, there are also times when the wind funnels up this valley and ruffles the waters with fury, baiting the paddler to compete for progress and twisting the bow of the canoe from side to side with mischievous taunts of power.

Layer upon layer of sedimentary rocks rise steeply from the water, with cedar and birch clinging tenaciously to impoverished scraps of soil between the rocks. In winter and early spring these terraced limestone walls are decorated with giant icicles as water drips from between the strata and freezes. When the low winter sun strikes these formations it creates a sculptured wonderland of icy fantasy.

At the head of the gorge the river ends on a quiet, rock-rimmed pool. One might expect to find a spectacular waterfall in such a location, a cascade of misty waters providing a dramatic start to such a river. Instead, the river, which has travelled underground for 400 metres, gently fills the pool from below, as if reluctant to disturb the peaceful silence of this place. The visitor can disembark here and explore the hidden river, or enjoy the trails within the park, before making the leisurely downstream journey back to Warsaw.

A description and a map of the Warsaw Caves Conservation Area are provided on page 44 of this book. It is also possible to rent canoes from the park attendants during the summer months.

Highway 7 to the Canadian Pacific Railway Bridge

Another short trip starts from the bridge on Highway 7 near the village of Indian River. There is sufficient road allowance for parking and a short path down to the water on the south side of this bridge, where a canoe can be launched. The water under the bridge is extremely shallow but gives way to reasonable depth almost immediately. A pleasant evening paddle for 2 or 3 kilometres upstream provides some good birding territory among woods and farm pasture land.

Some of the land beside the river shows evidence of annual flooding and supports a rich variety of ferns in the moist soil. In the spring an abundance of fiddleheads can be found along the banks. Edible fiddleheads, which take their name from the tightly coiled emergent fronds that resemble a violin scroll, come from the ostrich fern. In the early spring the only evidence of this plant is the crisp, brown fruiting bodies from the previous years. The tender new fronds will be found coiled at their base. By summer the fronds of this fern can reach 3 metres in height.

Beyond the Canadian Pacific Railway bridge the river becomes shallow and is difficult to negotiate against a current of small swifts. This is a good point to turn around and head for home.

11

THE WARSAW CAVES

Kathy Reid, Otonabee Region Conservation Area

Spelunking, canoeing and picnicking are just three of the many varied outdoor recreational opportunities that await you at the Warsaw Caves Conservation Area.

The Warsaw Caves Conservation Area, nestled in the valley of the Indian River, is located just 32 kilometres east of Peterborough, north of the village of Warsaw (map ref. 0 16). The property covers a total area of 224 hectares. It is owned and operated by the Otonabee Region Conservation Authority and provides the community with recreational and outdoor educational opportunities throughout the seasons, while also providing for the protection of the natural resource base.

The geologic formations (caves and kettles) and the scenic lookout are the primary attractions of the Conservation Area. Thirteen kilometres of hiking trails will introduce you to the intriguing geologic history of the area and the beauty of this natural environment.

The rugged terrain and geologic features of the area are evidence of the mighty forces of the glacial river which existed here about 10,000 years ago. At that time, the Indian River served as the main hydrologic link between glacial lakes Algonquin and Iroquois. As it surged through the present valley, the powerful forces of erosion weakened the soft limestone rock, causing it to crack horizontally and vertically. Trapping the granite debris that was carried downstream from the Canadian Shield, whirlpools gouged bowl-shaped depressions in the soft limestone. As the glacial waters subsided, great slabs of limestone rock collapsed and circular depressions remained in the now exposed rock.

The sectioned hiking trail begins from the parking lot. The caves section is marked "C 1" (cave 1) to "C 7" (cave 7). The trail that leads you to the kettles and the lookout point is marked by "KL"; following the "P" markers will lead you back to the parking lot.

The caves section of the trail is a spelunker's (cave explorer's) delight! For safety and comfort, cave explorers are advised to wear well-worn clothing and sturdy footwear, and to take along a flashlight.

The caves vary in length from 120 metres to 300 metres. You may find it necessary at times to actually crawl in order to make your way through the caves. The ceiling of cave 2 contains many fossils, primarily of shellfish. Cave 4 is a glacier cave; its temperature remains relatively constant, between 0 and 2 degrees Celsius, throughout the year. It is not uncommon to find ice in cave 4 in mid-July!

As you approach caves 5 and 7, you may find a unique fern, the walking fern (*Camptosorus rhizophyllus*). It is justly named for its characteristic walk. Long, narrow, fine-pointed arching leaves, radiating from the rootstalk, sprout new plants once the leaves touch the soil. You will probably find a number of young ferns surrounding the parent plant. The walking fern is rare in Ontario and prefers a habitat of shade and moist limestone, characteristic of this conservation area.

Entrance to one of the caves

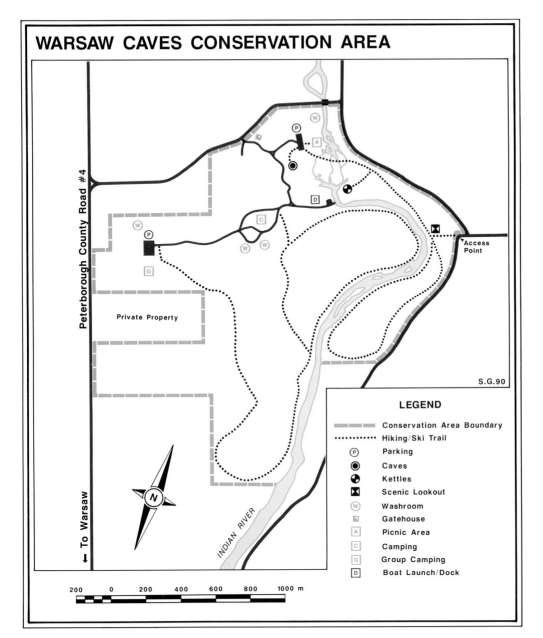

WARSAW CAVES CONSERVATION AREA

Peterborough County Road #4

← To Warsaw

Private Property

INDIAN RIVER

Access Point

S.G.90

LEGEND

▬ ▬ ▬	Conservation Area Boundary
··········	Hiking/Ski Trail
ⓟ	Parking
◉	Caves
◑	Kettles
☒	Scenic Lookout
ⓦ	Washroom
◹	Gatehouse
Ⓐ	Picnic Area
Ⓒ	Camping
Ⓖ	Group Camping
Ⓓ	Boat Launch/Dock

200 0 200 400 600 800 1000 m

Slow-growing eastern white cedar, eastern white pine, and white spruce cling to the shallow soils and exposed rock. Root systems search the crevices for water and nutrients while acting as a mechanical erosive factor in their own right.

The forest floor is covered in leaf litter and mosses, home to micro-organisms which work to break down the litter into humus.

The second section of the trail (to kettles and lookout) begins from the parking lot (so orient yourself to follow the caves trail back).

Numerous small potholes, or rockmills, are found along this section of the trail. The whirlpooling action of water and trapped granite was the force responsible for the creation of these bowl-shaped depressions. Many of them are no larger than a baseball in diameter.

Farther along the trail, you will hear rushing water, but you won't see any! At this point the Indian River flows through underground channels for approximately 400 metres. Once you reach the boardwalk, you will notice that the water reappears. The Indian River then continues to flow south to Rice Lake, and eventually into Lake Ontario.

The Indian River is a warm-water stream and provides habitat for smallmouth bass, yellow perch, walleye, muskellunge, and panfish.

From the boardwalk your hike continues to the kettles. There are 4 kettles; they look like overgrown potholes. The largest and most noticeable kettle measures 4.5 metres deep, 2 metres in diameter at the top, and 0.9 metres in diameter at the bottom. The three other kettles are partially or completely filled with forest debris. You will also notice that you are standing 9 metres above the level of the Indian River.

As you continue your hike to the lookout point you will see a variety of wildflowers. Gaywings, helleborine, hepatica, wild columbine, and goldenrod flower throughout the spring and summer seasons.

The lookout point offers a spectacular view of the Indian River Valley. It is hard to imagine that the peaceful valley was once the outlet of a glacial lake.

From the lookout point you may want to hike onwards along the trail, through cedar forest and open fields, or hike back to the parking lot area.

In winter cross-country ski trails are marked and groomed according to snow-cover conditions. The ski trails follow a different pattern than the hiking trail and take the skier into different areas of the property.

The Warsaw Caves Conservation Area is open to visitors year-round. For specific dates and hours of operation, be sure to contact the Conservation Authority. Opportunities and facilities exist for swimming, canoeing, picnicking, hiking, nature appreciation, and outdoor education. Arrangements can be made to serve groups of visitors by contacting the Conservation Authority.

Kettle, Warsaw Caves

Trail, Warsaw Caves

Mixed hardwood forest

12

TREES AND SHRUBS OF THE KAWARTHAS

Roger Jones and James Nighswander, Trent University

"On, on for hours, the same interminable forest stretched to the right and left, before and behind us," wrote Susanna Moodie in her book *Roughing It in the Bush*. She was describing a walk on a cold January day in 1839 to Dummer, which at that time was surrounded by forests. Moodie suggested that an apt name for her destination that day might have been "the last clearing in the world." One wonders whether Susanna Moodie would have believed that, as the 20th century draws to a close, the vast majority of people south of the Canadian Shield would need some form of motorized transport to get from the clearings to the bush!

Today the "bush" is not the daunting forest that confronted the pioneers a mere 150 to 160 years ago. Virtually all of the continuous primeval forest that once covered the Kawarthas has, in some way, been affected and altered by man. Much of the forest was cleared for farming, while large white pines and eastern hemlocks were felled for lumber. In some woodlots, it is still possible to find large rotting stumps of white pine or eastern hemlock and marvel at the magnificence of these trees prior to felling. Due to the demise of farming in areas where soils are poor and stony, abandoned fields can be seen in various stages of plant succession as they revert back to bush.

Abandoned fields are first colonized by weeds and then by trees such as white birch, eastern white cedar and trembling aspen, whose seeds are carried in by wind from mature trees. Another method of invasion is by suckers, which spread from trees already established along fence rows or in adjacent woodlots. In addition, there is now an aggressive colonization in some areas by introduced tree species such as black locust, European buckthorn and Scotch pine. Sadly, it appears unlikely that the kind of forest described by Susanna Moodie will ever become re-established.

The forests of the Kawarthas were originally moulded by geology, topography and by climatic changes during the millennia following the retreat of the last great glacial ice sheet, some 10,000 years ago. The pioneering plants which gained a foothold on the exposed land behind the retreating ice were tundra species. Then, as the climate warmed, seeds from trees growing to the south, safely beyond the detrimental effects of the ice sheet, slowly dispersed northwards, germinated, established themselves, matured and produced more seeds. Thus, slowly the land became colonized by succeeding species of trees and shrubs adapted to the warmer conditions that followed the retreating ice.

Tundra species were gradually replaced by a forest dominated by spruce trees, which were themselves largely replaced during the next 2,000 years, as the climate warmed, by other species which make up the modern mixed coniferous-hardwood forest. These included maple, beech, yellow

Fall colour

birch and hemlock. Some of the pollen produced by plants fell onto lakes, settled to the bottom and became part of the accumulating sediments. Today, sediment cores extracted from Kawartha lakes contain the fossil remains of pollen deposited hundreds or thousands of years ago, and with a microscope the parent plants of the pollen can be identified. By comparing the proportions of fossil pollen of different species, it is possible to reconstruct the kind of forest which existed in the past. As plant succession proceeded, decomposing leaves, branches and roots were mixed with mineral matter to give rise to soil whose nutrient value depended on factors such as geology, drainage and species of trees. Succession still continues, though for the past 175 years or so this natural process has been dramatically affected by man's activities, and presumably man will continue to have a great effect for the foreseeable future.

The Kawarthas are part of the mixed coniferous-hardwood forest which makes up the Great Lakes–St. Lawrence Forest Region, one of the great forest regions of Canada. This region lies between the Deciduous Forest Region of southwestern Ontario (the greater part of this forest extends south into the United States) and the vast Boreal Forest Region which spreads up through northern Ontario to the Arctic. The boundaries of these forest regions are not static, as evidenced by the presence in past warmer times of white and red pine up to James Bay. The Great Lakes–St. Lawrence Forest is typified on well-drained sites by a climax forest of sugar maple, yellow birch, beech and eastern hemlock. Burnham Woods, near Peterborough, is a good example of this self-renewing forest.

This forest, which once covered the Kawarthas south of the Canadian Shield, is today represented by small remnants in woodlots, conservation areas and provincial parks. All of these remnants are of a very mixed nature. Common hardwood trees occurring in the Kawarthas include maple, elm, beech, basswood, white birch, oak, ash and hornbeam. Evergreen species include white and red pine, balsam fir, eastern hemlock and eastern white cedar.

It is likely that the first impact of man on local forests occurred when Indians cleared areas where soils were suitable for maize (corn) cultivation. Dr. John McAndrews of the Royal Ontario Museum has suggested that white pine stands, which were reserved by law for the Royal Navy to make mast timbers, may have had their origins in such clearings. The major impact of man on the forest, however, occurred when European settlers began clearing the "bush" for farming, lumber and for browsing by farm animals. In this way much of the forest was inexorably altered and eventually lost. Large eastern white cedars were split for fence rails. White and red pine were felled for building materials. Eastern hemlock bark provided tannin, and various hardwoods were used for making fine furniture. Many sugar maple trees were saved for syrup production, so that farm woodlots became practically pure stands of this species.

Mark S. Burnham Provincial Park, on Hwy. 7 just east of Peterborough, is an example of the original mixed coniferous-hardwood forest of the Kawarthas. A stand of mixed hardwoods, with sugar maple, beech, basswood, ironwood and white ash, is present on the well-drained

upper areas of the park. Shrubs include leatherwood, alternate-leaved dogwood, and red-osier dogwood. Lower slopes in the park are inhabited by eastern hemlock (some at least 200 years old) and yellow birch. In areas where soils are more damp due to seasonal drainage, red maple, black ash and eastern white cedar thrive. There is evidence of the removal of a few large white pines from the woods, some of which were probably used in the construction of Burnham Mansion, located near the park.

A number of the tree species in the Kawarthas are at the edge of their range of distribution, meaning that these species are only found in isolated areas where environmental conditions are favourable. Several of these species typically grow further south, in the Deciduous Forest, while others live further north, in the Boreal Forest. Two examples of species which grow to a larger size further south are blue beech (*Carpinus caroliniana*) and bitternut hickory (*Carya cordiformis*). Blue beech is sometimes known as the muscle tree because its trunk has a smooth bark with ridges and furrows which can be felt just like muscles in a person's arms. A species more characteristic of the Boreal Forest is black spruce. In the Kawarthas it is found where there are remnant bogs, such as Cavan Bog. Other tree and shrub species have been introduced into our area and have almost become "weeds." An example of a tree "weed" is Scotch pine, often spreading from abandoned Christmas-tree plantations. A shrub "weed" is European buckthorn. European buckthorn is actually designated as a noxious weed because it is the alternate host of a rust (fungus) disease which attacks oats.

The seasonal colour variation of the mixed coniferous and broad-leaved foliage presents an ever-changing display of green shades in springtime and ends with the incredible autumnal blaze of the full spectrum of colour. The one native deciduous conifer, the tamarack, which borders swamps, presents a most delicate emerald green in early spring and punctuates the end of the growing season with splashes of golden orange. No man-made floral arrangement can rival the display of fall colour in the magnificent setting of the Kawartha Lakes, attracting viewers from far and wide every year.

Before we take it all for granted, it is well to remember that nature spent a millennia perfecting the forest and that in little more than a century modern man has done it irreparable damage. We are at last recognizing that the small amount of relatively undisturbed natural vegetation must be treated as a non-renewable resource if we are to preserve our natural heritage. Furthermore, the complex systems of young and old communities are now suffering assaults by an increasingly polluted atmosphere. It remains to be seen whether we are sufficiently concerned and committed to do something about it.

Poplars

Fall colour

49

Nogies Creek in summer

13

NOGIES CREEK BY CANOE

Terry Hunter

The northern part of Peterborough County is underlain for the most part with Precambrian rock formations. Because this area was scoured down to bedrock by the glaciers, it tends to be very rocky, heavily wooded and undeveloped agriculturally. Drainage is often poor, resulting in many wetlands, ponds, small lakes and streams.

Nogies Creek (map ref. P 18, on some maps called Harvey Brook) drains such an area, carrying its water southward into the north end of Pigeon Lake. Even though it is a small stream, it is able to maintain summer flow because of the water-holding capability of the type of terrain that it drains. Other streams with the same sort of drainage function are Squaw River, Mississauga River, Deer Bay Creek, Eels Creek and Crowe River. These streams release water southward into the Trent-Severn Waterway and are important for its successful summer operation.

Back in the lumbering days, these streams provided a means of transporting timber out of the largely inaccessible forest lands to the north. The streams were equipped with various dams, spillways and log chutes. Unlike the other streams, Nogies Creek is blessed with a major dam left over from the logging era. The dam is located about 5 kilometres upstream from the Highway 36 bridge, and it backs up the water about 7 kilometres, almost to Bass Lake. This provides convenient canoe access to a large wetland area which has not been encroached upon by development.

A very pleasant canoe trip can be taken on Nogies Creek starting at Bass Lake, which is located about 13 kilometres north of Pigeon Lake up the Bass Lake road. The road leaves Highway 36 near the Nogies Creek bridge and initially follows the west side of the creek. The flooded area of the creek is first visible about 5 kilometres north of Highway 36.

There are two places where a vehicle can be left for the end of the canoe trip. The first is at the Muskellunge Research Station building and the second is at the bridge which takes the road to the east side of the creek. The parking lot by the bridge marks the end of the snow-ploughed road in the wintertime. The road continues up the east side and, after passing several roads serving cottages, leads to the east bay of Bass Lake, where you will find a public landing with parking, outhouses and a wharf.

It is a leisurely 2-kilometre paddle down Bass Lake and into the large bay at the south end where Nogies Creek begins. A portage must be made around the Bass Lake rapids. The trail starts at the log boathouse and winds past the old bunkhouse that was used by the workers who built the Bass Lake dam to flood the rapids over 100 years ago. As the creek is approached, the water can be heard coming down the rapids and through the breach in the dam.

There is a short canoe trip down the creek and over a beaver dam to the next and last portage at the rock cut. As you step out of the canoe you will be aware of the water disappearing into cracks in the limestone. The lumbermen blasted a channel through the ridge to run their logs. The rock cut is flooded only during the spring run-off, and even then passage by canoe is treacherous. The portage is quite rough, but it is not very long. Once you are back in the water it is clear paddling for 5 to 7 kilometres, depending on where you intend to disembark.

The flooded creek below the rock cut is a Muskellunge Research Area and Sanctuary, and fishing is not permitted. Large specimens are often seen from the canoe. Largemouth and smallmouth bass have also been reported in good numbers. Otter, beaver, muskrat, mink and raccoon may be spotted along the creek. Deer, bear and snowshoe hare are plentiful in the woods.

Nogies Creek intersects ridges of crystalline limestone at an angle, resulting

Nogies Creek in winter

Morning mist on Nogies Creek

in a tortuous course. The ridge at the rock cut can be followed for about 3 kilometres. If the ridge is followed to the southwest for 2 kilometres, it will disappear under a limestone outlier. This outlier runs along the west side of Nogies Creek from Highway 36 to Bass Lake.

At one time most of Peterborough County was covered with limestone bedrock. The glaciers removed nearly all of it from the northern parts, exposing Precambrian rock. In places, patches of limestone remained intact and were termed outliers. Several of these are evident as one travels between Burleigh Falls and Bobcaygeon on Highway 36. The Nogies Creek outlier supports upland hardwoods with some white pine and cedar. This is in contrast to the scoured area of the creek where crystalline limestone is exposed and where the trees are predominantly softwoods, birch and poplar.

Returning to our canoe trip, about 200 metres below the rock cut you may get a glimpse of the walls of a log barn on your left. This barn was used to stable horses during the winter months when the area was logged. Around the next major bend the creek narrows and you will see a pile of rocks on the right shore. This pile is the remains of the tumbling dam, so named because it was less than 1 metre high and the logs were simply rolled over it. To the left, on the picturesque point under large white pine trees, stood the bunkhouse that was used by the loggers. Nothing remains of the bunkhouse and the 4-metre-long outhouse.

In the logging days a floating bridge spanned the creek near the tumbling dam. This bridge was needed to carry horses and lumberjacks to the other side, the ice on the creek being undependable and the water too deep to ford. The remains of the bridge can be seen downstream about 1 kilometre. It was made of pine poles 13 metres long and it was decked with maple boards, giving a width of 4 metres. When the logs were driven down the creek, the bridge was pulled along the shore to let them pass.

Below the tumbling dam the creek meanders around the crystalline limestone ridges, and sometimes the original channel is difficult to locate. About 1970 wild rice made its appearance at a few places on the creek. It has spread steadily since that time and is now found throughout the entire navigable length. In places the rice covers the creek completely, even where the water is 2 or 3 metres deep. (Ever paddle through a field of grain?) The rice is excellent feed for migrating waterfowl and it is usually all gone by the first of September.

At one point the flooded creek is nearly 0.5 kilometres in width. Further on you will see where Lavery Creek comes in from the east. The creek then narrows and is quite straight for over 1 kilometre. The Bass Lake road bridge is located in this section. Beyond the bridge the creek meanders again. Soon you will see the Muskellunge Research Station building on the right. This is the most convenient place to end a canoe trip. There is still 1 kilometre of good paddling to the dam but access is limited.

There are a number of interesting sites near Nogies Creek. One, located about 1.5 kilometre east, takes the form of a Precambrian rock outcrop about 70 metres high. From the top of this formation there is a panoramic

Spring canoeing

view for 5 to 15 kilometres. A few years ago there was an attempt to put a ski tow on this hill, and as you climb the slope you will be surprised to find steel pipes "growing" among the trees. Immediately west of the Nogies Creek outlier, near the north end, is a pit where marl was mined for the manufacture of cement early in this century.

The vegetation in the Nogies Creek area varies greatly with the soil, rock and water conditions. On the creek are a large number of black ash trees which have been standing dead since the area was flooded. Along the creek are large stands of white cedar, white pine and hemlock. Over the past few years there has been a significant dieback of white spruce and balsam fir. White birch and poplar are scarce near the creek as a result of beaver activity.

There are very few elms left now as a result of Dutch elm disease; you can see the remains of a rock elm stand at the rock cut.

The Nogies Creek outlier supports hard maple, beech, white ash, ironwood, basswood, black cherry and butternut. There are very few oak trees in the area. Under the hardwoods grow a myriad of wildflowers, including hepatica, wild leek and trillium. Some of the wildflowers seen along the creek include closed gentian, turtlehead, high bush cranberry, spikenard, fringed polygala, clintonia, yellow lady's-slipper, trillium, jack-in-the-pulpit and cardinal flower.

Nogies Creek runs through both Crown and patented lands, so use this waterway with respect for the property owners as well as the sensitive environment.

14

A RIVERSIDE WALK

Gordon Berry

The Nassua Mills Road, County Road 32, from Peterborough to Lakefield, provides a delightful scenic drive, cycle ride or walk on a summer afternoon. This road is known locally as the River Road, and this name is most appropriate, for it follows the river as it placidly meanders through a gentle valley. In the past this river presented a very different view. Rapids challenged the canoeist at many places, and when the Trent Canal was built in 1904, it required a total of 7 locks, between

Iris

Lakefield and Little Lake in Peterborough, to raise or lower the boats a total of 42 metres.

For those who like to bicycle or walk, the distance from Peterborough to Lakefield is approximately 10 kilometres. The Trent-Severn Waterway has developed some delightful, picturesque and well-kept picnic spots around the locks for the enjoyment of visitors by land or water; these locations make excellent spots to rest and enjoy the river.

The banks, for the most part, are shaded by cedars and abound with chickadees. In wider, slower stretches of the river, reeds and rushes provide habitat for redwing blackbirds. The occasional osprey and flocks of Canada geese can be seen during migration periods. The road provides excellent viewing of waterfowl, and the amusing spring mating rituals of some species of ducks are worth a trip for that purpose alone.

In May there are a few patches of coltsfoot in the gravel beside the road. These primitive flowers can easily be mistaken for dandelions from the car, but are worth a closer look if the season is right. Coltsfoot was introduced from Europe and the juices from this plant were used by pioneers to make coltsfoot jelly, candy and tea, which were believed to be beneficial in the treatment of colds.

A short circular walking route can be taken between locks 22 and 23, or between the university foot bridge and lock 23. It is possible to cross the river at locks 22 and 23 and make a short but pleasant walk using both sides of the river.

If you start at lock 23, cross by the narrow footway along the tops of the lock gates onto the island and walk north towards the dam. Cross the dam to the far shore and turn south or downstream. Caution: the dam is not designed as a bridge and children should only cross under strict supervision. There are loosely covered slots in the dam where logs are placed to control the water levels, and the sides of the dam have only minimum railings. If sensible use of the crossing is made and the caution signs are observed, there is no real cause for concern.

The land on the far side of the river is privately owned. The major portion is Trent University property and the part around lock 23 is owned by Susan and Bruce Crofts, whose comfortable bed and breakfast accommodation overlooks this stretch of the river. There is a courtesy sign asking users to avoid damage to the fence that keeps their animals in. It is to be hoped that all users will respect this request and keep their property free from litter. The generosity of private land owners who allow public use of their property cannot be too strongly stressed.

The trail, which follows the river towards Trent University, passes through some abandoned meadows and some shady, arching white cedar woods. In late August this path is bright with both summer and first fall flowers. White gentian and blue bottle, or closed gentian, nestle along the river margin. The delicate white filigree of Queen Anne's lace rises above the brown-tinged grasses, goldenrod and asters. Soft pale-blue clusters of chicory and spikes of viper's bugloss make a gentle counterpoint of colour against the pink of joe-pye weed and the white of boneset. The rich red candles of staghorn sumac and garlands of wild grape trim the edges of the woodlot, while platoons of cattails are marshalled in the wet places.

You can recross the river by the dam at lock 22 or continue along beside the university parking lot and through the campus to use the concrete footbridge that spans the river near the library.

As you return towards your starting point, beside the river there are young elms that have survived the Dutch elm disease of a decade ago. The abandoned railroad track can be used as an alternative route back to lock 23 or the walker can use the road that clings to the river bank.

Above: Swans in snow
Below: Spider

15

MILLER CREEK CONSERVATION AREA

Geoffrey Carpentier

Marshlands throughout Ontario are being drained and reclaimed at an alarming rate. Close to the city of Peterborough, at least one large wetland is being preserved and protected. The Otonabee Region Conservation Authority manages a 997-hectare site on the 7th Line of Smith Township. Drive east from Bridgenorth (map ref. N 17) on East Communication Road, which bends and becomes the 7th Line. The entrance to the area is on the south side of the road about a kilometre east of the town.

Officially, the area is known as the Snelgrove Brook Wetland, but locally it is called Miller Creek. The site

Marsh hawk

encompasses a variety of habitats, making it a productive and interesting wildlife area.

Much of the Kawartha area was once heavily glaciated. The passing of these ice masses not only affected the physical contours of the land, but also the underlying soil structure. Lying within the Peterborough drumlin field, which covers much of the southern part of the county, the wetland is underlain with sand, poorly drained peat and sedimentary limestone. Miller Creek bisects the area in a southwest to northeast direction. At some time in the past, the creek was dredged for part of its length adjacent to agricultural lands and scrub forest. However, at one point, the creek pans out over a wide area, creating the Miller Creek marsh, which dominates the attention of the visitor. Several other, smaller wetlands are to be found on the property as well.

For the botanist, the numerous vegetation zones in the area offers almost unlimited possibilities for study. Upland hardwood and mixed community stands, lowland wet and dry coniferous woods, grassland, late-stage bog, and of course sedge and cattail marshes crisscross the land. This diversity naturally means that one would find a large variety of plants. In addition to the more common and perhaps mundane species, many

interesting plants are to be found. These include, but are not limited to, ram's-head lady's-slipper, several species of clubmosses, goldenthread, starflower, one-flowered pyrola, Solomon's seal, jack-in-the-pulpit, skunk cabbage, baneberry, and thimbleweed, to name a few. Certainly the potential for study of individual species is there, but more interestingly, one can investigate the interaction of different plants within a community that is still progressing from an ecological standpoint.

Mammal fanciers, both vocational and amateur, can study a large diversity of animals attracted to the varied habitat and readily available water supply. Many of these species are used to humans, and may be quite approachable or at least tolerant of man's presence. White-tailed deer, muskrat, beaver, red fox, coyote, river otter, several weasels, European hare, eastern cottontail, star-nosed mole and several species of mice, squirrels and bats abound in their chosen haunts.

Herpetologists will not be disappointed with the variety of snakes, toads and salamanders, including the locally uncommon mudpuppy.

The birder, likewise, has many opportunities to pursue his or her hobby. A large percentage of the birds to be found in the Kawarthas occur here, either as migrants, winter residents, or breeding species. Many warblers, flycatchers, swallows, blackbirds, wrens, ducks, sparrows, hawks, and herons have chosen this area to breed. Shorebirds, more waterfowl and innumerable songbirds augment local populations during the spring and fall migration periods, stopping to feed on the rich food supplies. Winter species are thinly scattered and comprised mostly of sparrows, finches, hawks and chickadees. Several locally rare species have been sighted over the years. Sandhill crane, western tanager and sedge wren are included in this number.

Canoeists will find the possibilities somewhat limited, but certainly in the spring, when water levels are high, one can travel long distances along the creek, exploring usually inaccessible regions.

Photographers will experience countless opportunities to document the plants, animals and scenery.

Even at night, one can enjoy the area, listening for owls, frogs and toads, or simply stargazing.

The Otonabee Region Conservation Authority has developed long-range plans for the area that will undoubtedly enhance the use of the site. A nature-viewing platform has been constructed on the north edge of the marsh at one of the major access points. The tower offers novices and experts an opportunity to gain insight into the lives of the area's wildlife by observing the day-to-day activities of the residents. Improved trails, interpretive displays, day-use areas, special programs, and water management and habitat improvement projects are slated for the Miller Creek wetland and surrounding forests. Whatever your interests, you will surely find something fascinating at Miller Creek.

Green frog

Red-winged blackbird nest

Some examples of fossils found near Peterborough

Bryozoans or moss animals
Fossilized tubes of calcium carbonate that contained colonies of tiny organisms. The tubes branched internally and externally, forming lacy patterns. These organisms lived on the ocean floor and fed by filtering particles from the water. Small segments of these organisms are common in the slabs of sedimentary limestone around Peterborough.

Brachiopods or lamp shells
Formed of two unequal plates, each side being symmetrical. The two sides were hinged and closed by muscles. These organisms also lived on the bottom and fed by filtering organic particles for food. Common locally.

Pelecypods or clams
Similar to brachiopods, found in both fresh and salt water. These had hinged sides held together by muscles and each possessed a foot that could be extended between the sides and to enable them to move like modern clams. Siphons brought in food from the surrounding water. They often buried in the sand or mud.

Gastropods or snails
Conical or spiral shells, either flat or raised cones. Lived on the bottom of the ocean or attached to rocks. Fed on plants, debris and other animals. Many small examples in the limestone along the River Road.

Trilobites
Now extinct. Primitive arthropods rather like a modern sow bug or a wood louse. Comprised of a head, segmented trunk and tail. The body usually has three ridges. These bottom-dwelling marine organisms swam or crawled, and fed on loose debris. Uncommon in this area, but a few fine specimens have been found near Lakefield.

Crinoids or sea lilies
Marine animals that attached to the sea bottom, except for a few species that were free swimming. Comprised of a stem with a branching flower-like head. The stem often fragments into small flat discs. The discs show distinct five-part symmetry and vary greatly in design. These fossils are often quite large, about 30 centimetres in many cases.

16

FOSSILS

A Glimpse of the Past in the Present

Gordon Berry

Almost any trip to the places around Peterborough where the limestone is exposed will yield, to even the casual observer, a treasure of moulds, casts and impressions made by small organisms from the past. Curiosity about these small creatures from early times is readily aroused and many questions spring to mind. How old are they? How did they get here? What are they?

Between 400 million and 500 million years ago, all Ontario lay beneath a vast inland sea. During this time the sea changed constantly, growing and shrinking as the earth's crust moved and the land rose and fell. These seas were warm and shallow and supported a rich variety of marine life. A steady rain of sandy sediments, vegetation and dead marine life settled on the sea bed. The eroded land debris formed shales and the bodies of countless marine organisms formed limestone.

For a fossil to be formed it must possess hard parts of bone or shell; it must be buried quickly, before decay can set in; and then it must be left undisturbed for the long process of fossilization to take place. Most fossils in the Peterborough area were formed when a shelled organism became trapped and created a depression in the mounting sediment. Over a long period of time, water slowly dissolved the shell and left a hollow space. Minerals later filled this mould and a cast of the original shape was formed.

No one knows how thick the layers of limestone were originally, but with the passing of time, upthrusts from below and changes on the surface, such as the advancing and receding ice ages, first raised and then scraped away the upper layers of sedimentary rocks. Today, the maximum thickness in some areas is about 120 metres, although it is much less around Peterborough. The last ice age in this region departed a mere 10,000 years ago, and there has been little time for soil to accumulate on the surface of the limestone. As a result, wherever the blanket of topsoil is pulled back, or where a river, road or quarry has been cut into the surface, we are allowed a glimpse of the past.

The Otonabee River has carved a shallow trench and exposed several layers of limestone. As you walk along the river bank you can see the very shallow layer of soil on the top and then a number of layers of limestone reaching down to the water level. Further downstream, below the small hydro dam, just south of Thomas A. Stewart Secondary School, when the river is low and the water shallow, you can see the flat sheets of rock stretching across the river bottom.

The limestone along the banks of the Otonabee River is rich in small fossils. The most common forms are invertebrate fossils (organisms without backbones) such as brachiopods, bryozoans and crinoids. The soft internal bodies of these creatures have long since disappeared, but their hard shells have lasted or formed casts which display their former patterns.

The River Road, County Road 32, follows the river bank from Peterborough to Lakefield and provides many places where the limestone is exposed. Most of the fossils are trapped in sheets of sediment displaying dozens of forms in a few square centimetres. The majority are only partially exposed, with much of their detail obscured. Sometimes a search for fossils in the gravelly basins along the margin of the river can be rewarding. Here slabs of limestone have broken free during the spring run-off and been chipped and crushed, freeing small fossils among the gravel.

Most of the fossils you find will be small and broken; small wonder, they have lasted more than 450 million years and have been subjected to the abrasive action of water, wind, sun and ice.

A hammer and a flat chisel can be used to advantage with slabs of limestone. Set the rock on edge, place the chisel parallel to the face, give it a few sharp

Small local fossils

taps with a hammer, and the slab will fall into two thinner sheets of rock, exposing the layers of fossil impressions within. Thousands of species of fossils have been discovered in Ontario. Some cephalopods (squid-like creatures) found in nearby Hastings County are nearly 1.5 metres in length. The fossils along the River Road are, with the exception of some of the crinoid forms, usually less than 2 centimetres in length. A few trilobites more than 10 centimetres in length have been found near Lakefield.

There are two excellent quarry sites near the Otonabee River. The old Canada Cement Company plant, which ceased production in 1930, is still standing, and its tall smokestack is an easy landmark as you approach Lakefield. The quarry used by the company is on the east side of the river about 0.5 kilometres from the plant, just off Highway 134. A nearby road cut, also on Highway 134, provides good fossil hunting, especially in spring, when the work of winter ice

and water exposes new areas of rock. Another small quarry is located on Highway 28 about 5 kilometres north of Peterborough.

There is a small collection of fossils, with some good specimens, at the Centennial Museum in Peterborough. Trent University also has a small collection, while the Royal Ontario Museum holds a number of excellent specimens collected in this area.

17

TRENT UNIVERSITY NATURE AREAS

John Marsh and Rosita Ben-Oliel, Trent University

Trent University is located on the northern edge of Peterborough adjacent to Highway 28 and straddling the Otonabee River (map ref. N 17). It is fortunate to have a large (557-hectare), attractive, relatively natural and ecologically diverse campus. Since the university's beginning in the 1960s, 150 hectares on the east side of the campus have been recognized as a wildlife sanctuary. This sanctuary has been managed to protect it for field research, environmental education, and appropriate recreation. In 1989, an inventory of the university's natural assets led to the identification of an additional 15 nature areas on the campus (see map). Accordingly, the university has recognized these in its new plan for the campus, agreed to protect them, and established a nature areas committee to guide their management. As in the past, they will afford members of the university and the community many opportunities for environmental research, outdoor education, and nature-based outdoor education. As the university and local population expand and development increases, these nature areas will become increasingly valuable and worthy of our respect. The following information provides some details on the individual areas, as well as some guidelines for their use.

1. The Wildlife Sanctuary includes several drumlins and intervening wetlands. The uplands are typical of old field and early successional habitats with grasses, flowers, and scattered apple, hawthorn and aspen trees. The lowlands feature dense stands of eastern white cedar, marsh species, and some open ponds. Many birds species inhabit the sanctuary, notably great horned owls, performing American woodcock, and the rare Cooper's hawk. Mammals that can be observed include white-tailed deer, porcupine, raccoon, and red and grey squirrels. Several trails originating in a parking lot on Pioneer Road provide access for hiking and skiing in the sanctuary.

2. The nature area extending from Pioneer Road toward the Trent Canal includes a great diversity of biological communities. The northern part has a small stream containing the only known beaver dam on the campus.

Raccoon

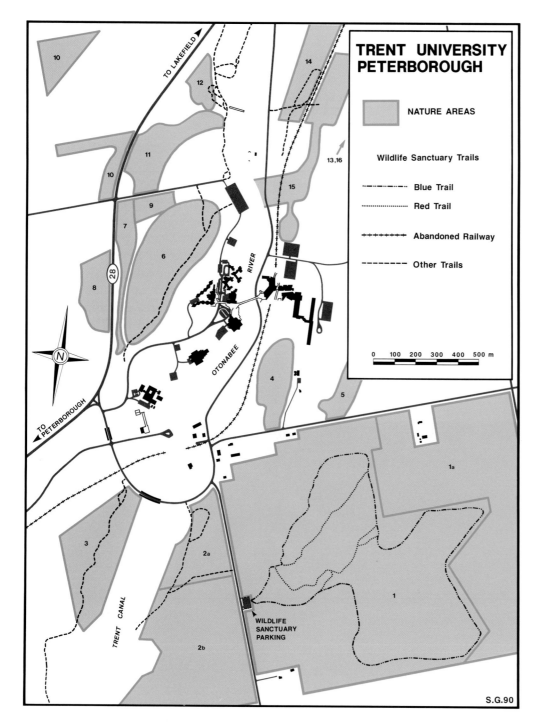

TRENT UNIVERSITY PETERBOROUGH

NATURE AREAS

Wildlife Sanctuary Trails

—·—·—·— Blue Trail

············ Red Trail

+++++++ Abandoned Railway

— — — — Other Trails

0 100 200 300 400 500 m

TO LAKEFIELD

TO PETERBOROUGH

OTONABEE RIVER

TRENT CANAL

WILDLIFE SANCTUARY PARKING

S.G.90

Some larger sugar maple, basswood, red oak, white ash, and ironwood trees can be seen along former fence rows. The southern part consists mainly of open fields being colonized by dense white cedar. Fauna of special interest include deer, beaver, frogs, great blue heron, belted kingfisher, and over 76 species of butterflies. Several trails penetrate the area, affording views over the Otonabee Valley and canal wetlands.

3. The south drumlin located west of the canal features woodlands and clearings. In the northwest, numerous trembling aspen have reproduced vegetatively to form clonal groups that come into leaf at different times and have contrasting fall colours. A wide variety of birds have been seen here, such as vireos, pileated woodpeckers, and the locally rare yellow-billed cuckoo. The area is accessible from the footpath along the canal.

4. The Archaeological Centre wetland has a permanent open-water pond fringed by a marsh and trees. The pond contains frogs, toads, spring peepers, blue-spotted salamanders and one species of fish. Near the pond is a snake hibernaculum where hundreds of garter snakes overwinter and breed.

5. The wetland east of Otonabee College consists of a sheltered stream and several ponds. Here are many wetland plants, some with rather unusual names: boneset, joe-pye weed, monkeyflower, and marsh skullcap. Muskrats and voles are also found, and in the spring one can listen for frogs, snipe and woodcock.

6. The Lady Eaton Drumlin, rising to 252 metres, dominates the campus buildings to the east. Its size shows the capacity of ice sheets to transport and deposit materials, while its steepness is

evidence of subsequent water erosion. The vegetation includes pine plantations, deciduous trees, notably the largest bitternut hickory on campus, and attractive ground species such as trillium, goldenrod and aster. A trail runs over the drumlin, offering great views across the valley.

7. The area along Highway 28 includes a small stream, wetland, and scattered trees. Among the interesting and attractive species are sensitive ferns, marsh marigold, red-winged blackbirds, and the common yellowthroat. The area is visible and accessible from the highway or drumlin.

8. The hardwood forest on the steep slope west of Highway 28 includes some of the largest beech trees on campus, maple trees that have been tapped for syrup, and a ground cover with various berries, including wild strawberry, gooseberry and red elderberry.

9. The forest north of the drumlin has an interesting mixture of upland and lowland tree and ground-cover species. Of particular note are the locally rare nut-bearing butternut trees and various ferns. Deer and woodland birds, like the black-capped chickadee and eastern wood pewee can be found here.

10. The abandoned Total Loss Farm, in the northwest corner of the campus, comprises a stream, wood, wetland, and fields. There are many moisture-loving plants, including the rare spikenard, and deer frequent the area.

11. The area east of Highway 28 and north of Woodland Drive includes a stream, pond, wetland and wood. Here one can see impressive stands of tall ostrich ferns and rough horsetail, and the royal fern, which is rare south of the Canadian Shield.

12. The woods west of lock 22 are dominated by mature maple and beech. As elsewhere on the campus, the ground cover includes introduced species such as black currant and Japanese knotweed. A rare Cooper's hawk has been observed here on several occasions.

13. The wetland on the west side of the 9th Line of Douro contains a small pond fringed by sedges and mature white cedars. The pond sustains seven species of amphibians, as well as dragonflies, and is visited by numerous songbirds.

14. Promise Rock Woods, west of locks 22 and 23, contains six conifer species, including some unusually large and impressive eastern white pine. The wood provides habitat for birds such as the great horned owl, downy woodpecker and several species not observed elsewhere on campus. A trail leads through the woods and past a limestone outcrop named, for a reason yet to be discovered, "Promise Rock."

15. The spring-fed wetland near the abandoned railway line at the northern end of the campus comprises a series of ponds linked by wet meadows. The permanent water affords habitat for late-breeding and maturing amphibians, such as green frogs, and the dense cattails attract muskrat.

16. A maple-beech grove is located south of the junction of the 9th Line of Douro and the Nassua Mills Road. The trees are uncommonly large, one maple having a diameter of 112 centimetres, reflecting the open environment which has been grazed by cattle. Grey squirrels, meadow voles, chipmunks, and nesting great horned owls have been observed here.

These brief descriptions reveal something of the ecological wealth and importance of the campus. More interesting

Flying squirrel

Marsh marigolds

habitats and species will no doubt be discovered as exploration continues.

The university believes it should protect yet encourage the appreciation of its nature areas. Accordingly, people are welcome to explore these areas provided they observe the regulations necessary for their protection, appreciation and scientific use. The following are prohibited: entrance to areas identified as closed, access by machines and vehicles, camping, fires, firearms, removal of plants or animals, littering, dogs, and most competitive sports.

The university welcomes questions, suggestions and information on these nature areas. Please contact the authors or the Chair, Nature Areas Committee, Trent University, Peterborough, K9J 7B8.

18

TWO CITY WALKS

Conrad Hill

Peterborough is fortunate in its location on the Otonabee River and Little Lake, as these features provide a very pleasant natural setting for walks within the city limits. Two city walks, outlined here, provide a wealth of waterside scenery with surprisingly little walking on paved city streets.

Circle walk around Little Lake

This is a 6-kilometre walk offering delightful views of Little Lake and the Centennial Fountain from many different vantage points.

Maple flowers

The walk starts from Rogers Cove on Maria Street in East City. Those who know the city may choose to start the walk at any of the many convenient locations mentioned along the way.

Walk east (to the left when facing the lake) along the beach to the canal lock, cross the lock gates and follow a path near the lake, behind the Trent-Severn Waterway headquarters building, into Beavermead Park. This well-kept stretch of parkland boasts some fine old willows, as well as ash and silver maple trees. Park benches provide a chance to enjoy some charming views of the city on the far side of the lake, as well the opportunity to watch the various pleasure craft that enter the canal.

After passing over a wooden arched footbridge which crosses a small creek, you will come to a paved park road. Turn left onto the road and follow it to the entrance of Beavermead Park.

Outside the park, turn right onto Ashburnham Drive and walk along the wide grassy strip outside the park fence until you reach Lansdowne Street, then turn right onto the sidewalk that leads toward the city. Cross the bridge over the Otonabee River, turn right on the first street and walk to the cemetery entrance.

If the gates are open, you have the option of going through the cemetery to the lake or following the fence around the cemetery. The cemetery is in a beautiful location on a point of land jutting out into Little Lake. Fine old shady maples provide a riot of colour in the fall, and these are gently accented by plantings of blue spruce and mountain ash. This is a good location to watch birds in the migration seasons and the wild and domesticated waterfowl on Little Lake.

Follow the lakeshore along Crescent Street to the Art Gallery. The gallery has new shows each month, as well as a permanent collection of pictures and a rent-a-picture program. The gallery adjoins Crary Park, with its concert stage, marina and restaurant.

Follow the shoreline around the marina docks and the Brownsea Sea Scout Base and cross over the wooden arched footbridge into the Holiday Inn parking lot.

Behind the Holiday Inn is a floating walkway that eventually leads to the railway bridge across the Otonabee River. Cross the tracks and you will find a walkway on the left side of the bridge that will bring you to the east side of the river.

From the bridge you can look upstream to the Quaker Oats plant and the graceful arches of the Hunter Street bridge, the longest non-reinforced concrete span in the world.

After crossing the bridge, turn right and follow the grassy strip beside the river and along the margin of the lake until you again meet the railway tracks near Maria Street. Turn right and in a few hundred metres you will return to the Rogers Cove parking lot.

Trent Canal and Otonabee River Walk

Start at the Rogers Cove parking lot and follow the beach east (to your left when facing the lake) until you reach the canal.

Follow the grassy banks of the canal to the lift locks. The small but excellent Trent-Severn Waterway visitors' centre, just below the locks, describes many aspects of the construction and operation of these historic locks.

Cross Hunter Street into the small park area beside the locks. Take the path that runs northeast up some

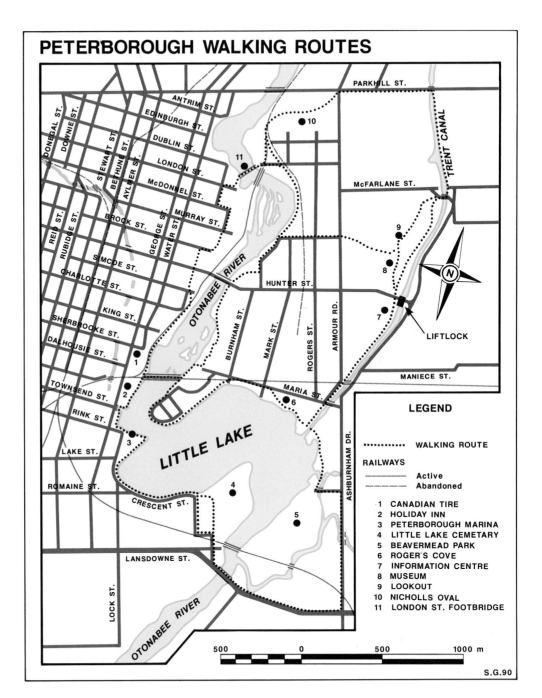

PETERBOROUGH WALKING ROUTES

LEGEND

············· WALKING ROUTE

RAILWAYS
——— Active
— — — Abandoned

1 CANADIAN TIRE
2 HOLIDAY INN
3 PETERBOROUGH MARINA
4 LITTLE LAKE CEMETARY
5 BEAVERMEAD PARK
6 ROGER'S COVE
7 INFORMATION CENTRE
8 MUSEUM
9 LOOKOUT
10 NICHOLLS OVAL
11 LONDON ST. FOOTBRIDGE

S.G.90

concrete steps and meets a paved road leading to the Lookout. The Lookout commands an almost 360-degree view over the city of Peterborough and surrounding countryside. Close by is the Centennial Museum, which is also well worth a visit. At the north end of the Lookout parking lot, a path leads downhill to the High Level Bridge. Take this path, cross to the other side of the canal, and follow the east bank of the canal to Parkhill Road.

While we associate wildflowers with undeveloped areas rather than city walks, many parts of this trail provide an abundance of wildflowers. Many of these flowers are so common we give little heed to their colour and beauty. Dandelions and buttercups, wild parsley and Queen Anne's lace, milkweed, bladder campion, saxifrage, cinquefoil, fleabane, chicory, a variety of clovers and vetch, as well as a profusion of the many species of asters and goldenrod may be seen. In addition, there are many other wildflowers along the banks and a host of aquatic plants in the water.

At Parkhill Road turn left and cross the canal again, continue along the road to the traffic lights at Armour Road. Cross the road and enter Nichols Oval park. Heading in the same general direction, cross the park until you reach an abandoned railbed or the banks of the Otonabee River. Turn left and follow a path beside the river, which meets with a paved path by the blue London Street footbridge. (The footbridge offers an alternative route back into the city.)

Continue south, on the same side of the river, to Douro Street and follow Driscoll Terrace to the entrance of the Quaker Oats parking lot. Go down the hill behind the Quaker office and pass under the Hunter Street bridge. Follow the paved road past the ball park and onto Engleburn Avenue. Turn right on Engleburn Avenue and go to Maria Street. Here you can turn left and follow Maria Street back to the Rogers Cove parking lot, or you can turn right and follow a path to the railway bridge and cross the river to the Canadian Tire or Holiday Inn parking lots.

Fountain, Little Lake

66

19

ALONG JACKSON CREEK

Clay Vardy

A walk down the old railroad right-of-way along Jackson Creek from Ackison Road to Jackson Park can be very rewarding, especially during spring and fall. The area can be reached by driving west from Peterborough on Parkhill Road to Ackison Road, then turning north and driving about 800 metres until you cross the old railroad (the tracks have been removed, but the former crossing is easily recognized). Park on the hard shoulder north of the old crossing and walk east toward the city on the railbed.

The first kilometre or so is an area of swamp and thickets. It is home to blue-winged teal and mallards from spring through fall. Green-backed herons can frequently be seen flying over or sitting quietly in the trees. During spring and fall many migrant species can be found in the bushes on either side of the track. Sometimes these bushes are alive with birds, including many species of warblers, such as redstart, black-throated green, blackburnian, parula and mourning. White-throated and white-crowned sparrows and various other songbirds may be seen and heard.

Nesting birds to be found during the summer include kingbird, song and swamp sparrows, red-winged blackbird, yellow warbler and common yellowthroat.

The path next brings you to a grove of cedars and, on the left, to Lily Lake. Although not directly accessible, Lily Lake can be viewed from the railbed. Kingfishers and great blue herons may be seen fishing on the lake. During spring and summer, sora and Virginia rails may be heard calling at dawn and dusk.

Passing beyond Lily Lake, the track follows Jackson Creek for about 2 kilometres and leads into Jackson Park. This is a very pleasant walk along the banks of Jackson Creek through an area of cedar. During spring and fall migration, many species of warblers, sparrows, thrushes, and flycatchers may be seen.

Summer residents include black and white warblers, ovenbirds, and veery.

Although much quieter, with few birds, a walk along the track in winter can be very rewarding. The section between Lily Lake and Jackson Park is especially beautiful in winter, and some winters, cardinals are found in abundance. Throughout the entire walk, many tracks may be recognizable in the snow, including those of rabbit, squirrel and mink. With some luck, you may even see the animals themselves.

This area is not one of the best-known natural areas of Peterborough. As such, it can provide a pleasant, quiet walk at any time of the year.

Pine grosbeak

Monarch

Tiger swallowtails

Atlantis fritillary

Bronze copper

20

WATCHING BUTTERFLIES

Phil Schappert

The Kawarthas offer a wide variety of activities for the field naturalist to enjoy. A personal favourite is watching butterflies. In much the same way as people watch birds, I watch butterflies.

Watching butterflies is often even more enjoyable than bird-watching: butterfly-watchers are rarely required to be up at the crack of dawn or be out on one of those blustery, cold, wet, grey days! Both hobbies are very similar. They involve the pursuit of colourful flying animals. Activities such as monitoring numbers, recording behaviour, keeping lists of species encountered, and even gardening for the purpose of attracting your favourite species, invite direct comparisons to bird-watching. Other activities, like learning to identify the larval food plants, having an appreciation for communities where particular butterflies may be found, and knowing the life-cycle variations and flight periods of specific butterflies, have more in common with wildflowers and "botanizing."

Butterfly-watchers in the Kawarthas may, with luck, timing and diligence, encounter about one-half of the butterflies which occur in Ontario. These include representatives of species typical of both more northern and more southern regions. Many different plant communities and topographic features — the result of "sitting on the edge" of the Canadian Shield — are responsible for the region's diverse butterfly fauna.

There are two main considerations which you, as a butterfly-watcher, should keep in mind when planning your outings: the time of the year and the type of habitat you'll be investigating. Like both birds and wildflowers, butterflies are usually found at particular seasons. Half of the battle is knowing when to look.

The height of butterfly season in the Kawarthas is late June and early July. The entire season runs from early April through late September but often includes finding a mourning cloak flying in mid-March (while there's still snow on the ground) or seeing a Compton's tortoiseshell still on the wing in early November!

Many of the northern species are single-brooded. This means that they are often found only in May. Examples of such ephemeral species include the mustard white, the olympia marblewing, the elfins, the chryxus arctic, and the roadside and pepper-and-salt skippers. Other species of northern character may be found flying with the majority of species in early summer.

Species which may be found late in the season, in late August or September, are often of southern affinity. These include the second or third broods of the monarch, the sulphurs, the cabbage white, the inornate ringlet, and the pearl crescent. Most other species will be encountered around the height of the season.

Like most wildflowers or some birds, butterflies are often found only in specific habitats. The second half of the battle is knowing where to look.

It is not generally useful to look for wood warblers in old fields or for daisies in the woods! A parallel for butterflies would be looking in a cow pasture for a butterfly whose caterpillar feeds on marsh grasses!

The available field guides and natural history books about butterflies (see the references section at the back of the book) will not only help you to identify the species that you see here, they will also offer hints on where to look for them. In most cases plant communities will offer clues to the butterflies which may be found there.

The best butterfly-watching occurs at habitat edges, where fields and woods meet, or at the edge of the marsh. This region is blessed with a multitude of habitat edges. All that remains is for you to pick one and get out there! To help you find productive spots, I've included a short list of some of my favourite locations throughout the region.

In the south, check the campus and nature sanctuary of Trent University, especially the Lady Eaton Drumlin (between Lady Eaton College and Highway 28) and alongside the canal east of the South Drumlin (see the article on Nature Areas at Trent for a map). The areas around the Cavan Swamp or the Sawer Creek Conservation Areas, the countryside east of Lang, and the region just north of Peterborough Airport (south of Highway 115) are often productive.

In the north, some of my favourite areas include the east end of Stoney

Olympia marblewing

Lake, especially the Petroglyphs Provincial Park, the Twin Lakes area (Peterborough County Road 46 north of Havelock), the Warsaw Caves Conservation Area, Highway 36 between Burleigh Falls and Buckhorn, the area around Glen Alda, and the Galway-Cavendish Forest Access Road south of Catchacoma.

The butterflies which you can expect to see, in addition to those already mentioned, include the tiger and eastern black swallowtails, the spring azure (look in late April at Mark S.

Little wood satyr

Burnham Provincial Park), the red and the white admirals, the viceroy, the comma, the question mark, the little wood satyr, the American painted lady, and hobomok and European skippers. These species can be found throughout the region.

In the south, look for the northern cloudywing (try the campus of Trent University in early June), the duskywings, the arctic, least, tawny-edged, and dun skippers, the bronze copper, the Acadian hairstreak, the eastern tailed and silvery blues, the great spangled, aphrodite, silver-bordered, and meadow fritillaries, the Baltimore, Milbert's tortoiseshell, and the large wood nymph.

In the north, seek out the dion skipper (this species may be found around some of the marshes in Petroglyphs Provincial Park), the pink-edged sulphur, the Atlantis fritillary, Harris's checkerspot, and the northern pearly eye, in addition to the ephemeral species already mentioned. Many of the southern species can also be found in some areas of the north.

The current trend towards watching and photographing butterflies instead of capturing and killing them is long overdue (it's not too late for us to learn something from those birders after all!). A good mix might include careful netting of a specimen for close examination, then releasing it unharmed. Try that with a bird and a handnet! If you learn to enjoy just watching butterflies, then there will always be more of them for you, and your children, to watch again another day. Good hunting and have fun!

21

MARK S. BURNHAM PROVINCIAL PARK

Wade Scorns

Situated at the southeast corner of the Peterborough city limits, this 44-hectare tract of virgin woodland contains many different species of trees and a wide variety of wildflowers, plants, birds, and small mammals.

The land was originally owned by Zaccheus Burnham in 1837, and was preserved by the Burnham family in its natural state. After the death of Mark Burnham (great-grandson of Zaccheus), his wife presented the land to the Ontario government as a provincial park in 1957.

Located on Highway 7, 0.5 kilometres east of Television Road, this park is for day use only, with no admittance fee. Facilities consist of parking, picnic tables, barbecue stands, rest rooms, and picnic shelters.

At the end of the parking lot there is a large billboard with a map of the park. The 1.5-kilometre nature trail forms a figure-8 loop with a by-pass at midpoint so there is a shorter walk available. It is advisable to walk up the west side of the trail; however, this involves climbing a steep hill at the north end. Those who seek easier walking should follow the eastern route so they can then descend this hill on the return trip.

At the starting point of the west trail, there is an impressive stand of mature eastern hemlock intermixed with beech, yellow birch, and sugar maple trees. In the spring, before the forest floor is shaded by the leafy canopy, one can find both red and white trilliums, wild leek, wild lily of the valley, false and star-flowered Solomon's seal, wild ginger, jack-in-the-pulpit, rose twisted stalk, round and sharp-lobed hepatica, clintonia, trout lily, large-flowered bellwort, spring beauty, and Canada violet, along with northern white violet. Most of these wildflowers can be found in varying degrees along the entire trail. There also can be found nesting blue jays, American robin, red-eyed vireo, white and red-breasted nuthatches, rose-breasted grosbeak, scarlet tanager, wood thrush, and broad-winged hawk.

Just 200 metres further on, there is a split in the path. To the right there is a mixture of hardwood species consisting of yellow birch, red maple, beech, hop hornbeam, white ash, ironwood, basswood and sugar maple. In this area the ovenbird can be heard more easily than seen. This section of the woodland is a regular breeding area for both the downy and the hairy woodpecker. A

Mark S. Burnham Provincial Park

Pileated woodpecker

Park in winter

treat to look for is the magnificent pileated woodpecker, a regular visitor and breeding bird in the park since 1984.

Two other woodpeckers that may be seen foraging in this area are the northern flicker and the red-headed woodpecker.

Another bird that breeds in this section is the great crested flycatcher.

Along the main outside loop of the trail, the woodland becomes distinctly divided. On the left, eastern hemlock predominate until the halfway point of the trail, and the forest floor is nearly devoid of underbrush. On the right or east side of the path, there is a mixture of trees and a considerable variation in landforms. Here porcupines, raccoons, chipmunks, grey squirrels and garter snakes can be found in varying numbers. One flower worthy of special mention is Indian pipe. This saprophytic plant is totally white and contains no chlorophyll at all. There are many examples of this flower to be found in the moist leaf litter on the west side of the trail.

At the northern end of the loop is a low-lying wet area where with careful searching you may find American woodcock, ruffed grouse and veery. This is the site of the steep hill mentioned earlier. The trees here are a mixture of eastern hemlock, beech and yellow birch. Black-capped chickadees nest in this area, along with bluejays, scarlet tanagers, wood thrush and red-breasted nuthatches. On the top of the hill the trees change to hardwood once again. Near the intersection of the two paths there is a nest built by a red-tailed hawk. Look for a basswood tree marked with a sign stating the age of the tree as 140 years; due east of this tree the hawk may be seen attending to its nest.

For those individuals who might like a more vigorous outing, there is a wooded swamp to the west of the nature trail. This wetland is within the park boundaries. The water level depends on the amount of rainfall received during the hottest and driest summer months. During the first half of the 1980s the water level averaged 1 metre; in the summer of 1988 there was no water to be found anywhere! Needless to say, the waterfowl and other birds that feed and breed in this area were almost non-existent during this dry period. Several species of salamander may be found among the leaves and rocks in this area.

The terrain is flat, with sinkholes in the western section when water is plentiful. There are numerous little islands of dry land. On these are the nests of red-winged blackbirds, common grackles, northern waterthrush, common yellowthroats, and white-throated sparrows. European starlings, common flickers and yellow-bellied sapsuckers have been seen entering and exiting cavities, suggesting nesting activity. The brown creeper has been seen here in the breeding season, although no nest has been found behind loose bark. This swamp is a good place to find green herons, with as many as six seen in a short stroll. Great blue herons may also be seen, usually one to three. The heron will often stand still, so have the camera ready. Once in a while, with a little luck, you may find an American bittern standing in its camouflage position, quite still with its bill pointing up. The waterfowl most often found are Canada geese, mallard ducks, blue-winged teal, and the occasional wood duck.

Some of the common wildflowers in the marsh are bur marigold, marsh marigold, spotted touch-me-not, orange hawkweed and nightshade. The two most uncommon flowering plants to grow here are the skunk cabbage and white turtlehead.

22

SPRING ECSTASY

Gordon Berry

When winter rolls back the blankets of snow and Nature prepares for its annual spring festival of flowers, there is a special exuberance and excitement in the air. Each day, as the sun climbs higher into the sky and its warm rays seek out the last patches of snow and ice in the secret parts of the forest, the meltwater seeps into the soil to free the icebound roots from their winter fetters.

Available water is the spring alarm clock that awakens the plant from its winter dormancy. Water re-starts the plants' osmotic pumps to send the sap and water, laden with nutrients, surging through the vascular tissues, bringing new life to dormant cells. Abundant water supplies crack seed coats to initiate germination. It also swells to bursting the hard protective tissues that have sheltered tiny embryonic leaves all winter long. Increasing warmth spurs the activity and, in just a few days, trees and shrubs are decked in fresh green mantles of leaves and they develop a canopy of shade that limits the amount of light reaching the woodland floor.

The many small flowers that carpet the woods in spring have a few short weeks, between the time the snow melts to provide water and the leafing out of the tree canopy, to produce their flowers and enjoy a brief period of frantic activity in the warm spring sunshine.

Most spring flowers achieve this timing miracle by storing energy over winter in their bulbs, tubers and roots, in readiness for the spring rush. Their sensitive cells respond not only to the warmth and available water, but also to the short hours of daylight and long nights (photoperiod) to adjust their biorhythmic clocks and initiate flowering.

Even before the snow has melted, skunk cabbage, a speckled red, melon-sized helmet-like flower has, by its cellular activity, melted the snow in bucket-sized depressions. When flowering is almost done, the first fresh lime-green leaves appear around the flower.

Hepatica, which takes its name from its liver-coloured and liver-shaped leaves, also thrusts its hairy stems anxiously through the crisp leaf litter while snow patches can often still be seen in the cooler parts of the wood. It opens its delicate blue, white or pink flowers before its new season

Wake-robin

Top row, left to right: Indian pipe, Cardinal flower, Spring beauty. Bottom row, left to right: White turtlehead, Bloodroot.

leaves have unfurled. In early times plants that reminded people of a particular organ in the body were often believed to hold medicinal properties for the treatment of ailments of that particular organ. Such was the case with hepatica.

Coltsfoot is often casually mistaken for the dandelion, as it has a similar sized and coloured flower. It is found along gravelly roadsides or on muddy banks. It has a most distinctive stem which is made up of overlapping segments. The leaves, which appear after flowering is almost complete, are the size and shape of an impression made by a colt's foot, hence its name.

The pure white blossoms of bloodroot, with their collars of deeply lobed green leaves, are found in spreading patches. Their tuberous roots run underground, raising new plants at the nodes of these underground stems. The name is associated with the rich red juices that flow from any break in the plant and particularly from the root. This was a common dye much loved by the early pioneers. The Indians also used bloodroot juices to dye clothing and possibly to paint their faces.

In marshy areas the golden marsh marigolds provide splashes of yellow sunshine against the black earth. The dark-green leaves make an excellent substitute for spinach, in fact the stems, leaves and buds all provide a rich spring vitamin source.

A favourite spring flower is the tiny spring beauty with its delicate semi-transparent petals and tracery of fine pink veins. These small blossoms are sensitive to cold and respond to sudden drops in temperature by closing their flowers tightly.

Skunk cabbage

Like many of the early spring blossoms, wood anemones are white. There are several species of anemones, but the most common produces a single flower some 10 to 25 centimetres above the ground. Soft breezes gently sway the slender stems and cause the movement that gives them another common name, windflower.

Violets appear in a variety of white, blue and yellow colours and colonize a wide range of habitats. Some species, such as the pansy, have been cultivated for garden use, and others are loved for their delicate fragrance.

Trout lily (it blooms at the start of the trout season), or adder's tongue, is found in moist woods and along stream banks. Often it nestles among the roots of trees and makes a bright splash of colour against the rough texture of darker bark. Another name for this yellow flower is the dogtooth violet, although it is not a violet at all. It produces single, elongated bell-like

flowers that droop above two mottled leaves that look as if they have been washed in soapy water and never rinsed.

The provincial flower of Ontario is the trillium, and it is perhaps the best known of all Ontario flowers. While there are several varieties of trillium, they all have the same characteristic number pattern of threes in their leaves, petals, sepals, or multiples of three in their stamens. Hence the prefix "tri" in its name. The large white trillium is the most common variety and the purity of its white petals may often turn to a blush of pink as the blossom fades. The red trillium is called wake robin locally and it has a less than pleasant odour. For this reason it is known in some areas as wet-dog trillium or stinking Willie. Less common, but also found in the Kawarthas, are the rose-centred

Clockwise, from top left: Coltsfoot, Violet, Painted trillium, Green trillium.

painted trillium and trilliums with variegated green and white petals.

Another favourite spring flower is the tiny rose-pink gaywing, or fringed polygala, that carpets some local woods in May. It is also known as flowering wintergreen. This flower belongs to the wintergreen family and the roots produce a rich wintergreen fragrance when crushed. The more common white-flowered wintergreen, that, as its name suggests, stays green all winter, bears small red waxy berries. The crushed leaves and edible berries produce a pleasant aromatic flavour which will be easily recognized from candy of the same name.

The bright red and yellow flowers of the wild columbine are found in both open and shaded ground, often in inhospitable stony places. Its feathery foliage of mitten-shaped leaves support the gentle pendant blooms comprised of five tubular pointed spurs. Its Latin name, *Aquilegia*, has a possible derivation from the Latin word *aquila* (eagle), as the flower has a fanciful similarity to the clawed foot of this bird.

The foamy white flowers of the wild lily of the valley have two leaves per stem, with a cluster of small flowers at the apex. False Solomon's seal has similar-shaped leaves, which alternate along an arching stem, and also has a cluster of creamy white flowers at the tip. The true Solomon's seal has similar leaves but has pairs of yellow flowers hanging along the stem at and between the axils and the leaf nodes.

The time when these spring flowers may be enjoyed is all too brief. It is a time when insects are appearing in bothersome numbers, many to assist in the pollination of these flowers, and a time when gardeners are preparing the ground for planting and a host of post-winter chores are vying for attention. Yet these short days of spring can justly claim a favoured place in the hearts of nature lovers everywhere. The woods and fields are never more beautiful, never more fresh, more active or alive with birdsong than in spring. Practise the art of procrastination on the chores and indulge the spirit. Resist the fast-paced demands of modern living and enjoy the free prescription that is the best of all medicines for the cares and stresses of life: a spring walk in one if our local woods, such as Mark S. Burnham Provincial Park, Heber Rogers Wildlife Area or Peter's Woods. Feel the ecstasy that is spring.

23

LANG PIONEER VILLAGE 1820-1899

Margaret MacKelvie

Nestled in the Lang Valley by the Indian River, Lang Pioneer Village features over 20 restored and furnished homes and other buildings originally constructed between 1820 and 1899. The village is situated on a 10-hectare site between two restored, historic water-powered mills, the Lang Grist Mill, built of stone in 1846, and the Hope Sawmill, restored to 1875. Friendly villagers of all ages, dressed in authentic historical costume, go about their daily chores, gardening, baking, tending the animals and visiting the General Store to shop and collect their mail. Sparks fly from the anvil in the blacksmith's shop, handbills are printed on the old press in the Register Print Shop and the gentle smell of wood smoke fills the air. Chat with the village carpenter at his treadle lathe or the spinner at her wheel, and visit the 14-room Keene Hotel for cool cider, lemonade or afternoon tea. All contribute to the authenticity of this living museum village experience.

The first settlers arrived in Peterborough County in 1818 and had to build their own homes and communities. Many were ill-prepared for this new experience. They had to cut down the trees and create clearings for their log homes. At Lang Pioneer Village visitors can see the kinds of log homes the settlers would have built and the development of a backwoods community with a store, church, school, blacksmith's shop, township hall, print shop, barns, carpenter's shop, hotel and stone flour mill.

Lang Pioneer Village was established by the County of Peterborough in 1967 to preserve the history of the area. Since then, thousands of visitors have taken the trip back in time and discovered how the pioneers lived. The village is complete with lanes and pathways, farm animals, rail fences, vegetable and herb gardens, hitching posts for horses, a village dock on the Indian River, and other authentic details of a 19th-century hamlet.

Lang Pioneer Village is the site of David Fife's 1820s log cabin. Fife, who at the age of 15 emigrated from Scotland to Canada, was one of the first farmers who realized that the European strains of wheat were not suited to the Canadian climate. He wrote to a friend back home for new seed samples and began a horticultural experiment which led to the discovery of Red Fife wheat in 1842. It soon became popular in southern Ontario and the northern United States because of its high yields and excellent breadmaking qualities. By 1870, Red Fife was well established on the Canadian Prairies, and during the next 30 years, it was regarded as the best variety of spring wheat.

Red Fife wheat was ground into flour at the three-storey Lang Grist Mill. The limestone for the walls of this impressive structure came from the Indian River. On special-event days during the season, whole-wheat flour is ground at this mill, which was built in 1846 by Thomas Short.

While Lang Pioneer Village is open from early May to late October, the 650-square-metre Lang Visitor Centre, built in 1983, offers year-round visitor and museum programs, and is said to be one of the finest museum facilities of its kind. It houses a museum exhibit gallery, visitor reception area, multi-purpose room for meetings, craft workshops, environmentally controlled facilities for archives, artifact storage, a conservation laboratory and other work areas. A gift shop in the Lang Centre specializes in locally made handicrafts and has a fine selection of books of interest to all ages.

Throughout the year there are special days featured in season — sheep shearing, a Victorian flower show, pioneer contests, corn roasts, cider-making, harvest festivals, 1880s Christmas Festival, dogsledding and many more. At these special times groups of craftspeople, dancers, musicians, and others with a wide variety of skills bring their talents to Lang to revive traditional customs and activities.

The area on which the village was built was originally a cedar swamp. One can expect to find, along the river bank, those flowers which flourish in dampness. In the meadow there are a number of different varieties of "meadow" flowers. Great blue herons can be found from spring to fall, often with their young, and recently Canada geese have been breeding in the area. One note of caution: beware of the poison ivy in the river area.

Fall colour

24

BIRDING IN THE KAWARTHAS

Geoffrey Carpentier

The Kawarthas are unique in that birds are concentrated here in all seasons, for all to enjoy. For birds, the year is divided by their activities into four seasons, which are different from the ones which people recognize. The winter season begins in October or November and lasts to April or May. The breeding season runs from late May to July. The spring and fall migration periods occupy the rest of the year.

The Breeding Season

The Peterborough area is bisected by a major geological feature called the Precambrian Shield. To the north, deep lakes and rivers, coniferous forest, bogs and a boreal flavour of birdlife dominate. Many species of thrushes, ducks, hawks and warblers, including the provincially rare prairie warbler, annually breed in this area. These species are usually difficult to find as nesters elsewhere in southern Ontario.

The southern half of the area has an agricultural flair. Remnant woodlots, extensive marshes and swamps (particularly along the Rice Lake shoreline) and fields support the cumulative species list for the region. Open-field birds, such as meadowlarks, bobolinks and a myriad of sparrows, take advantage of the available habitat in these manipulated areas. Finally, urban sites provide nesting areas for a handful of species that favour these locations. The diversity of nesting habitats has led to 157 species of birds being identified as breeding species in the Kawarthas.

Migration Periods

The spring and fall migration periods can be most exciting as vast numbers of birds stream overhead, either north or southbound, to breed or to escape the pressures of winter. During these periods, birds need safe sites to rest and feed. There are many significant spots in the area that these birds utilize. Waterbirds take advantage of

Black-capped chickadee

the numerous marshes, lakes and rivers. Several sewage lagoons provide harbourages for shorebirds. Gulls congregate at some of our landfill sites, while the small passerines (warblers, vireos and thrushes) overflow our parks, woodlands and hedgerows. Sparrows, finches and hawks rest in the fields and remnant woodlots.

Winter

This season is generally assumed to be a lifeless time of year. Snow and cold blanket our area. But winter can be an exciting time for bird study. Many

Bald eagle

species arrive only in early winter, often in large flocks, and spend several months. Snow buntings, bohemian waxwings, tree sparrows, pine grosbeaks, crossbills and redpolls visit annually. Additionally, a variety of diving ducks use our many open-water areas for feeding and resting. Unexpected species show up regularly at this time of year. Some of the best finds include indigo bunting, Lincoln's sparrow, scarlet tanager, pine warbler, Harris' sparrow, tufted titmouse, Barrow's golden-eye, harlequin duck and northern mockingbird. The Petroglyphs and Nephton areas annually host seven to ten bald eagles and two or three golden eagles. These birds follow the wintering deer herds, feeding on the carcasses left by wolf kills.

Three hundred and nine species have been recorded in the area over the years. Included in this number are several extremely rare species: swallow-tailed kite, spotted redshank, western tanager, western kingbird, blue grosbeak, black-headed grosbeak, Bell's vireo, Clark's nutcracker and the only Canadian record of a broad-billed hummingbird.

Bird-watching

Choosing a site to observe birds becomes a simple task when one realizes that birds are truly everywhere! Every field, yard, park, woodlot and marsh has birds. Naturally, some areas are better than others, but your quest will be directed by your need to see a few special species or a wider variety. Certainly, any outing can be successful if one just takes the time to appreciate whatever is around. Some of the better birding sites within the area include: Jackson Park (city of Peterborough), Miller Creek Conservation Area, the Lakefield Marshes, the Rice Lake

Top row, left to right: Screech owl, Scarlet tanager. Middle row: Mourning dove, Killdeer. Bottom row: Loon on nest, Canada goose on nest.

Marshes, Warsaw, Serpent Mounds Provincial Park, Lake Katchawanooka (winter), Squirrel Creek Conservation Area, Petroglyphs Provincial Park, Millbrook, Eels Creek, Lasswade (winter), Birdsall Beach, Cavan Bog, Villiers, and the sewage lagoons at Lindsay, Lakefield, Port Perry and Havelock.

A strong nucleus of competent birders, who will act as leaders and teachers for organized outings, is approachable through local nature clubs. Many of these same people are extremely active and involved with several local bird-oriented projects, including the Ontario Heronry Survey, the Ontario Loon Survey, the Rare Breeding Bird Project, Bluebird Nestbox Projects and Christmas Bird Counts.

Whether one decides to study birds as a vocation, a consuming pastime or simply as a hobby, it is essential to learn as much as possible about their preferred habitat, food, behaviour, life history, songs, and the like. Libraries, field guides and fellow naturalists will be of paramount assistance in this regard.

Good luck and good birding.

Top row, left to right: Barred owl, Eastern bluebird. Middle row, left to right: Scarlet tanager, Great grey owl. Bottom row: Heronry.

25

THE KEN REID CONSERVATION AREA

Denise Lauzon, Kawartha Region Conservation Authority

Located 5 kilometres north of the town of Lindsay, the Ken Reid Conservation Area offers visitors a variety of natural experiences (map ref. N 19).

Owned and managed by the Kawartha Region Conservation Authority, the property was acquired because of its diverse landscape, central location, and biologically significant adjacent wetland. The 7 kilometres of gently sloping trails wind through an interesting blend of open meadows, mixed forest and marshes. This variety of habitats makes the area an ideal location at which to spend a relaxing afternoon during any season.

During the winter months, the property has groomed and track-set trails for cross-country skiers. Flocks of chickadees cluster among the groves of evergreens, blanketed by freshly fallen snow, and flitter among the tall branches. An abundance of animal tracks crisscross your path. Snowshoe hares, red squirrels, ruffed grouse, fox, white-footed mice, porcupines and white-tailed deer are all active residents of the sheltering forest.

On weekends, the stillness of the area may be disturbed by the sounds of dogsled teams racing along the roadway throughout the property. These races provide an excellent opportunity to watch the beautiful Siberian huskies in action as man and dog strain together to cover the distance.

With the arrival of the warm spring weather and longer days, the area is transformed from a quiet winter wonderland to a busy natural area where plants and animals begin the process of revitalization and reproduction. Spring wildflowers, including trilliums, goldthread, hepaticas, lily of the valley, and violets, blanket the forest floor. In the open meadows, the newly arrived migratory birds, which include meadowlarks, bobolinks and bluebirds are busy establishing territories and gathering nesting materials.

The trail system consists of two trails. *The Blue Trail* starting at the first parking lot, meanders for most of the 2 kilometres through a dense mixed forest consisting of balsam fir, white pine, cedar, poplar and birch. A short portion of the trail borders the McLaren Creek marsh and allows the visitor to sit at the viewing platform and watch the nesting osprey, or walk along a boardwalk constructed through a section of the marsh. Walking at a leisurely pace, the Blue Trail will take the average visitor about one hour to complete. The second trail, known as the *Orange Trail*, is approximately 3 kilometres long and borders marshes for most of its length. Winding through low-lying cedar forests and small open clearings, it also includes two smaller boardwalks. The Orange Trail will take the visitor approximately 1 1/2 hours to walk at a leisurely pace.

Several structures have been incorporated into the trail system to allow the visitor to experience diverse wetland areas. These structures include three boardwalks, a viewing platform and a canoe launch, all of which provide

Boardwalk at Ken Reid Conservation Area

access to the McLaren Creek marsh, which borders the northwest fringe of the conservation area. Marshes are bursting with the activity of muskrats, beavers, carp, perch, frogs, snakes, kingfishers, waterfowl, and osprey during the late spring and summer months.

The magnificent osprey has made this area its home since the late 1970s, after much effort on the part of local groups to erect suitable nesting platforms. The McLaren Creek marsh and adjacent Goose Bay area are unique in that they are believed to have the highest density of active osprey nests in any part of Ontario!

The viewing platform that overlooks this marsh provides an excellent opportunity to view two such nests. Osprey return to the same nest year after year, adding new sticks each breeding season. An average nest is 1 metre in diameter, and between 30 and 60 centimetres deep. Often, the tree or structure on which the nest is built collapses under the weight that has accumulated over the years.

Osprey feed primarily on fish. The occasional mammal, bird, reptile, amphibian, and invertebrate round out their diet. The feeding behaviour of osprey will fascinate even the most active youngster. Scanning the water from a height of 10 to 30 metres, the osprey hovers above a fish until it swims into a suitable position. Then, with incredible speed and agility, the osprey folds its wings upward and backward, and dives feet-forward into the water. Using its powerful wings, the osprey emerges with the fish secured in its strong talons. Before flying off to a feeding stump or branch, the osprey repositions the fish so that its head faces the direction into which the bird

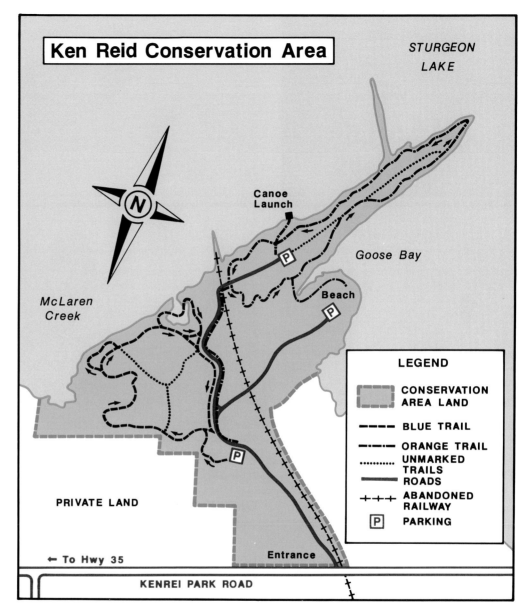

Ken Reid Conservation Area

STURGEON LAKE

Canoe Launch

Goose Bay

McLaren Creek

Beach

LEGEND

- - - CONSERVATION AREA LAND
- - - - BLUE TRAIL
- · - · ORANGE TRAIL
········ UNMARKED TRAILS
——— ROADS
+ + + ABANDONED RAILWAY
P PARKING

PRIVATE LAND

← To Hwy 35

Entrance

KENREI PARK ROAD

is flying. This technique serves to minimize wind resistance created by the prey, which may weigh up to 2 kilograms.

As the warm, hazy days of summer are replaced by the cool crispness of fall, many changes occur throughout the conservation area. The summer residents, including the osprey, embark on the long migratory flight south; flocks of waterfowl stop to feed and rest in the marsh; squirrels and chipmunks fervently continue to gather their winter supply of nuts and cones. Visitors to the property will also notice the changing tree foliage, the gradual transformation of the field flowers as they turn to seed, and the appearance of puffballs and other fungi on the damp, dark forest floor.

Whether it be winter, spring, summer or fall, take a morning or afternoon to visit the Ken Reid Conservation Area. The sights and sounds will surely make your visit a memorable one!

Other Kawartha Region Conservation Authority Properties

The Pigeon River Headwaters Conservation Area and the Fleetwood Creek Natural Area are located in the hills of Manvers Township, approximately 25 kilometres south of the town of Lindsay. These areas serve to protect unique natural features which include cold-water streams, valley lands and mature hardwood forests.

The Fleetwood Creek Natural Area is a 364-hectare parcel of land owned by the Ontario Heritage Foundation, but managed by the Kawartha Region Conservation Authority. Situated within the Oak Ridges Moraine glacial formation, this property includes spectacular scenic views, a population of re-introduced wild turkeys, a 500-year-old Indian village site, and grassland plants that are normally found on the prairies.

The Pigeon River Headwaters Conservation Area is a smaller property, 125 hectares in size. Its forests contain massive cherry, maple, birch, spruce and hemlock trees. The cold-water feeder streams support a healthy population of brook trout. An abundance of wildlife, including snowshoe hares, ruffed grouse, beaver and deer, also make use of the area.

26

KAWARTHA MARSHLANDS:
A Canoeing Naturalist's Paradise
Ed Reid

From our vantage on shore, the luminous oranges and purples of dawn are mirrored magnificently in the waters of the marsh. Black spikes and arches of rushes contrast sharply against the gathering light. The abrupt call of a green heron pierces the morning stillness — *Skiew. Skiew.*

The reflected colours break up as we set the bow of the canoe into the water. Alternating bands of light and dark move outward from the craft and explode into smaller radiating concentrics as they play off the bases of rushes.

The wetland gives the initial impression of chaos, owing to the sheer abundance and diversity of habitats, textures and forms. Underlying that appearance, however, is a complex natural order.

We had both been waiting for a morning like this for weeks — the opportunity to get up before dawn, escape the slumbering suburbs via empty roads, and revel in the awakening of the marsh. The canoe is the perfect medium for such a liaison.

The serenity of this marsh is imposing this early in the day, and we are conscious that we do not belong. An "inbetween" world, neither land nor open water, the wetland still belongs to Nature. She will let us in on some of its secrets, but only on her terms. We are silent.

We paddle slowly toward the bank of cattails. Our only sound is the rhythmic splashes of water droplets from our paddles as they glide into and out of the tepid water. The distant raucous cries of red-winged blackbirds grow in intensity. Suddenly, the water boils among the lily pads to our left. A swirling vortex is the only trace of the startled muskellunge. From the cattails we hear the broken-pump sound of an American bittern. *Gongh-ka-ongh. Gongh-ka-ongh.*

We are fortunate in the Peterborough and Kawartha area to have a wealth of easily accessible wetlands such as this. (Unfortunately many more marshes have been, and continue to be, lost to imprudent development in the Kawarthas and elsewhere in southern Ontario.)

Some of the best nature viewing, photography and general wilderness appreciation await those who venture into the marsh by canoe. This is certainly true for the Peterborough and Kawartha Lakes area.

The light is gathering quickly now. We paddle into an opening within the cattails and stop amidst a flotilla of water lilies to listen. The raucous cries of the blackbirds have increased considerably with our intrusion. One particularly perturbed male challenges us with a fine display of his crimson epaulets, scolding us while at the same time balancing precariously upon a straining cattail.

Further into the bay we see the vee-shaped wake made by a muskrat swimming toward his home in the cattails. Muskrats are the "builders" in the marsh, their handiwork consisting of cattail rafts built for feeding, trails cut through dense marsh, and numerous lodges. Some of the lodges are still in use, others have provided a

Water lily and rose pagonia

Marsh view

Canoeing in a wetland can be an invigorating educational experience. Far from "useless wastelands," as marshes were once considered by many, these wonderful ecosystems teem with life and beauty. For the uninitiated, a paddle in a marsh can be an awakening of the senses to the natural intrigue that surrounds us. Children especially seem to revel in this smorgasbord of sights and sounds.

With the canoe we can access only the most watery types of wetlands, the open water marshes. By land we can easily explore the edges of the opposite end of the wetland spectrum, the wooded swamp. In between often lies a rich gradient of much less accommodating wetland types — shrub carrs, sedge or cattail mats, or hummocked marshes with much water interspersion and little access. Each wetland type differs not only in hydrologic composition, but also in the habitat it provides for plant and animal communities.

For convenience, wetland types have been broken into marshes, swamps, fens and bogs (though in nature the distinctions are often unclear). In the Kawartha area we have many types of swamps, and marshes are still common along the shores of lakes and rivers. Bogs, characterized by sphagnum moss and black spruce, are much less common here, but often occur as small areas within larger marsh-swamp complexes. Where these sensitive bog or fen habitats occur, they usually harbour regionally rare plants. Pitcher plant, sundew, white bog orchis and grass pink are all common to local bogs, but rare within the region.

From our position in the canoe we develop a good sense for the rich diversity of the open-water marsh, itself

foothold for shrubs within the marsh, and still others are now used as nesting platforms by waterfowl and terns, or as shelters for voles, shrews and snakes.

Through the clamour of the blackbirds we distinguish the thin rattling song of the marsh wren, one of several less common birds we might encounter in the marsh this morning.

We take the opportunity to cast our fishing lines among the lilies, for the early morning marsh is a favourite haunt of largemouth bass.

The sun is moving overhead, and its penetrating rays have illuminated the active underwater world. Peering into the water on the shaded side of the canoe allows us a glimpse of the ethereal aquatic world. Here, we see

the bottom of the marsh carpeted with muskgrass and wild celery. Pondweeds and milfoil form tall columns and deep green caverns, cover for predators and prey alike. The water is alive with small organisms — waterboatmen, dragonflies, nymphs, water beetles, fish fry and minnows, leeches, and tadpoles — all engaged in a wonderful survival dance below the whirligigs on the surface. Pumpkinseed sunfish hover casually (or is it nervously?) beneath our canoe.

To our delight, the shrill *keeeek keek* of a black tern draws our attention back above the water's surface. Another tern appears, a mate we presume, and we move out down the edge of the marsh.

composed of several community types. Wild rice and water lilies grade into a community of arrowhead and pickerelweed that buffers the thick cattail marsh. Beyond the marsh we can see the transitional zone of cedar, sweetgale and dogwood shrubs where the marsh grades into a swamp community. We briefly sight a northern harrier hunting along the swamp edge.

Returning to the shore after spending the morning on the marsh, we feel refreshed. In a few short hours we have encountered more wildlife than we might have seen in weeks on the strictly terrestrial landscape. To know a wetland is to fall under its spell: to destroy it becomes unthinkable. Yet 50 to 75 percent of the Kawartha Lakes wetlands have been lost, and southern Ontario wetlands are still disappearing at a rate of 1 to 2 percent annually.

Fortunately, with increasing awareness of the importance of wetlands, and an emerging will to protect and restore these valuable habitats, wetland destruction is becoming far less acceptable.

Wetland exploration can be recreational, inspirational and educational. It can also be instrumental in helping save these valuable areas. Naturalists' records can play an important role in alerting the agencies entrusted with the protection of our natural heritage as to the composition and inhabitants of a specific wetland.

Below are outlined some of the most easily accessible marshlands in the Peterborough and Kawartha area. Most of these wetlands occur along the Trent-Severn Waterway and are public to canoeists. (Note: In some rare instances, anchoring a craft may be a trespass infraction!)

1. Lower Mississauga River
(map ref. O 17)

A dense riverine community of cattail, sedge, and low shrubs cradles the lower stretches of the river. Access is easy from Highway 36 just east of Buckhorn. Wetland vegetation exhibits some fen characteristics. Raptors, herons, waterfowl and songbirds are abundant along this easily paddled section. It is the terminal portion of a local canoe route.

2. Wolf Island Complex
(map ref. O 17)

A diverse marsh complex along the northeast shore of this designated provincial park at Lovesick Lake. Many shallow bays and open water inlets provide the canoeist with excellent wildlife viewing opportunities along a pristine shoreline. Access from above Burleigh Falls, with other small wetlands en route. Diverse bird community.

3. Lakefield Marsh
(map ref. O 17)

A rich labyrinth of emergent and submergent marsh communities in the southwest end of Lake Katchewanooka. Excellent nature viewing opportunities in this easily accessible wetland. Black tern, northern harrier, marsh wren and least bittern are among the many species of birds that inhabit this marsh.

4. Pigeon Lake Marshes
(map ref. N 18)

Several large floating cattail marshes exist along the southern and western shores of Pigeon Lake. There are excellent opportunities for nature viewing and fishing. Black tern, American bittern, sora, osprey and

marsh wren are recorded in these rich wetlands. The marsh south of Emily Park is easily accessible.

5. Indian River Mouth
(map ref. N 16)

A riverine community of dense cattail and low shrub swamp, it provides habitat for a variety of mammals, amphibians, reptiles, waterfowl and herons. Easily accessible from Keene, this portion of the river is also the terminal stretch of a local canoe route.

6. Bear Creek Marsh
(map ref. O 17)

A deep bay of Pigeon Lake 3 kilometres northwest of Gannon's Narrows at the mouth of Bear Creek, cradles a rich submergent/rice/cattail marsh community. Common loon, American bittern, black tern and osprey may be seen. There are other wetlands in adjacent bays, but there is heavy boat traffic.

7. Lower Otonabee River
(map ref. M 16)

There is a productive riverine swamp and marsh complex along the lower stretch of the river to Rice Lake. Public access from County Road 2. Easily navigable, with abundant wildlife viewing opportunities. Mammals, amphibians, reptiles, raptors, waterfowl and herons.

Many more fascinating marshlands are open to the canoeist in the Kawartha Lakes and the numerous lakes in the northern region of Peterborough County. Consult topographical maps and the Ministry of Natural Resources for more information about wetlands, canoe routes and public access.

27

THE EMILY TRACT

Rick Calhoun, Ministry of Natural Resources

About halfway between Lindsay and Peterborough a small chunk of mixed forest lies waiting to be discovered. The Emily Tract, a 78-hectare property which forms part of the Victoria County Agreement forest, is located on County Road 14 just west of its intersection with County Road 10 (map ref. N 18). The property is owned by Victoria County but is managed for both recreational and economic benefits by the Ministry of Natural Resources through an agreement which dates back to 1922.

Much of Victoria County was settled for the first time between 1820 and 1889. Early pioneers worked hard to tame the forest. Sometimes their efforts paid off, and they were able to develop prime agricultural land. In other cases, the land they intended to bring under the plough just wasn't suited to agricultural production. Such is the case with portions of the Emily Tract.

Typical of this part of Victoria County, the tract is made up of an interesting and impressive variety of landforms, including a predominant esker, steeply to gently rolling glacial moraine deposits, and a wetland. The soils in the area were formed about 12,000 years ago and consist of tills and well-drained, water-deposited materials, evidence of the retreating glacier.

The tract is comprised of a wide variety of vegetation. The forested areas are of two forms, natural mixed hardwood stands and introduced red and white pine plantations which date back to 1922. Upland areas display poplar, red maple, balsam fir, spruce and white birch, while tamarack, black ash, cedar, balsam fir and spruce dominate the lowland areas. In addition, towering red and majestic white pine dot the tract, clustering in some areas. About 8 hectares of the tract form Cowan's Bay, a locally significant wetland. This wetland area contains mainly cedar, alder, dogwood and grasses. Finally, much of the land surrounding the tract is made up of both active and abandoned agricultural fields.

The diversity of habitat in the Emily Tract has resulted in its use by an equally wide range of wildlife. Mammals found in the area include river otter, deer, beaver, raccoon and muskrat. Birdlife includes black terns, roosting owls, hawks, chickadees and nuthatches. The area may even be visited on occasion by the recently re-introduced wild turkey. The small stream which crosses the

Fox

Emily Tract

tract contains cool water and is inhabited by brook trout, with both bass and muskie just a short distance downstream.

A wide range of recreational opportunities exist within the tract. Throughout the entire year, one can enjoy light hiking, bird-watching and nature appreciation. Two 1-kilometre trail loops traverse the tract, exposing the visitor to its full range of terrain. Hiking is probably at its best in the mid to late spring, after some of the low-lying areas have dried up a bit. The sounds of birds and the fresh smells of spring fill the air, and all around you, plants and leaves begin to grow.

You can, of course, continue to enjoy the tract on foot throughout the summer months. Insect populations may be high in some areas, so appropriate clothing or protection is recommended. Once autumn begins, the trails become covered with layers of falling leaves. The sound of their rustling underfoot adds to the enjoyment of the tract at this time of year.

In the winter season, visitors can continue to walk throughout the area or they can use the trails to enjoy limited cross-country skiing. The rolling topography provides a number of short downhill runs and quick turns which add to the enjoyment.

Other forms of recreation within the tract include fishing and (between September 15 and December 15) hunting. Visitors to the tract during the hunting period are well advised to wear bright clothing and make their presence known. (Naturalist's note: I personally would visit at some other time!)

The Emily Tract is a wonderful place for you and your family to renew your relationship with nature. Its easy, well-marked hiking trails permit you to explore the area at all times of the year. If you are more adventurous, you can wander off the trail and discover the more remote parts of the tract, where some of the largest trees in Victoria County can be found. Come out and discover the wonder and beauty of nature at the Emily Tract.

EMILY PARK: THE MARSH BOARDWALK

Gordon Berry

Close to the Emily Tract is the Emily Provincial Park. This park lies along the shore of Pigeon Lake and is a popular camping place from spring to fall.

The park contains a short but interesting Marsh Boardwalk, which is especially convenient for families with young children. The trail is about 1 kilometre in length and at a leisurely pace takes about 30 minutes to cover. A trail guide is provided at the start of the walk, and its numbered paragraphs correspond to numbered posts along the way.

Marshes are special places, producing a rich variety of plants and organisms that are the basis of food chains that spread well beyond the limits of the marsh. The trail guide provides an excellent cross-section diagram of the marsh. This shows the type of vegetation that can be seen in each type of habitat, depending upon the depth of water present and height of the plants above the waterline.

Among the many features of this trail is a grove of green ash trees. The green ash was valued by Indians for the flexible characteristics of its wood, which they used to make frames for snowshoes, sleds and cradles, as well as bows and arrows.

A boardwalk extends across the shallow waters of the marsh and enables the visitor to examine more closely the marsh plants, duckweed, water lilies, American lotus, cattails, pickerelweed, and bur reed. Tadpoles and small fish swim among the plants, while painted turtles bask in the sun on rotting logs, and broods of wood ducks feed in the open stretches of water.

The trail ends on a sphagnum island with a lookout tower that provides an excellent view of an active osprey nest. Here you can watch the osprey feeding their young or making spectacular dives into the water to catch fish. Binoculars are a great advantage for viewing not only the osprey, but other birds and animals that may be seen from the viewing platform and boardwalk.

A decade or so ago the park was extensively replanted with a variety of trees. These trees have matured and now shade the campsites and roads within the park, providing privacy for both wildlife and campers, as well as beauty and a pleasing ambience throughout the park.

Emily Park

A COUNTRY WALK NEAR BETHANY

Murray Palmer

For a morning or afternoon of quiet contemplation and exercise, hiking or skiing the back roads through the rolling hills of Cavan Township near Bethany can be very rewarding. Most of the land beside the trail is posted against trespassing, but these byways offer good opportunities for nature-watching. This upland of mixed deciduous forest is home to many different kinds of trees and woodland plants, insects, birds and mammals.

The trail starts near the Devil's Elbow Ski Resort, which is on County Road 38 and well signed from both Bethany and Omemee. After passing the Devil's Elbow parking lot, take the second turn to the left. A short distance along, you will find a sandy road leading off to the right. Although unmarked, this is the west end of the 13th Line of Cavan Township. There is sufficient space beside the road to park without obstructing traffic.

At the start of the trail there is a beautiful woods on the right and a hayfield surrounding chalet-style homes on the left. Along the way you will see cultivated fields and mature woodlots, two ends of a succession cycle. Fields are kept at high productivity by farmers, but if left untended, even for a short time, they begin to revert to scrub woodland. These fields support a relatively limited variety of plants and animals. However, the climax forest of maple and birch has developed a wonderful diversity of flora and fauna that depends upon this stable habitat for food and shelter.

One family of birds that relies on the existence of mature forest is the woodpeckers, of which at least five species may be found here. You can recognize a woodpecker by its undulating flight pattern and, with experience, identify the species by the distinctive rhythm of its drumming. Drumming is the beating of the closed beak on a resonant surface of hollow wood. It serves the same purpose as song does for other birds, declaring occupation of territory and advertising for potential mates.

A conspicuous white rump patch on a brown-backed bird identifies a northern flicker when it flushes. Listen for its *wik-wik-wik* calls and the louder *cuk-cuk-cuk* of the spectacular crow-sized pileated woodpecker that chisels large, deep oblong holes as it searches for carpenter ants. The familiar downy and

Sumac

Top: Eastern bluebird.
Bottom: Red fox.

the larger hairy woodpeckers dig smaller conical holes to extract wood-boring insect larvae.

If you are lucky you may sight a red-headed woodpecker, the only species in eastern Canada having red on the entire head, neck and throat. This bird is quite uncommon but may be found in semi-open woods and meadow habitat.

A loud *kwee-urk* or a mew-like alarm call may alert you to a yellow-bellied sapsucker. When not hunting trunks

and branches for insects, including many pests, such as moths of the tent caterpillar, sapsuckers make rows of evenly spaced holes and collect with their brush-like tongues the oozing sap and the wasps, ants and flies attracted to these sap wells. Like the red-heads, sapsuckers also use the flycatcher technique to take flying insects.

Humans also take advantage of the rich sap of the sugar maple, and you can see an old sugar shack in the woods on the right side of the trail, where plastic collecting hoses link the trees. A few pioneer-style sap pails hung on spigots are still to be seen on the fringes of the woodlot and on isolated trees.

Eventually the road makes a left-hand turn, with another track leading uphill a little to the right. At this point you have two alternatives: you can turn left and enjoy the panoramic views before re-entering the woods, or proceed straight ahead up a somewhat rugged trail through some beautiful woods. In the spring, the ground below these maples is richly carpeted with wildflowers: hepatica, Dutchman's breeches, trilliums, Solomon's seal, wood violets and many others. This route is also a good place to find the tracks of raccoon, red fox, coyote, white-tailed deer and other mammals.

Turning left, a gravel road divides hayfields from old pastures. Here bountiful hedgerows of sumac, apple, cherry and hawthorn trees, and wild grape vines running along the cedar rail fences provide handy food and cover for meadow inhabitants.

The staghorn sumac, named for the soft fuzz that covers its new branches like velvet-clad antlers, is an essential survival food for many over-wintering

and migrant species of birds and mammals. This plant is high in nutrients at a time when little else is available. Held above the deepest snow, many of the red conical clusters of fruit remain uneaten until well into the spring, providing food for the early arriving eastern bluebird. Cottontail rabbits eat the bark, and white-tailed deer eat the fruit and stems.

Pioneers made a drink like lemonade from the crushed fruit of this plant, as well as rich dyes from its fruit and stems. Sumac is prized by carvers and woodturners, who delight in the colour and grain of its wood. In the autumn, these lightly foliated shrubs present a brilliant display of red leaves in colourful contrast to asters and goldenrod.

The sparse ground cover of the old pasture is excellent habitat in which eastern bluebirds can search for spiders, crickets, beetles and grasshoppers. Like red-headed woodpeckers, bluebirds are uncommon now. A widespread loss of nesting sites, caused by the removal of dead trees and old fence posts, and by competition from European house sparrows and starlings, together with the effects of pesticides and severe winters, have made their existence rather difficult. To encourage a recovery of these beneficial and attractive birds, members of the Peterborough Field Naturalists have erected wooden nesting boxes in nearby fields, and these have been successfully used for some years.

The road winds on to the 14th Line of Cavan, where there is a sign identifying the road you have just walked as Shield's Drive. You have now covered 4.2 kilometres and it is time to turn back.

30

MOSSES AND LICHENS

Tom Atkinson

On a Peterborough Field Naturalist trip many years ago, I remember our field-trip leader, Harry Williams, examining a small green patch on a decaying log. When asked, "Have you found a rare moss?" Harry replied, "No, but there are four mosses, four lichens and a liverwort here." We learned that passing over "the little green things" means missing a lot of interesting plants.

Lichens are "dual organisms" composed of two kinds of plants, an alga and a fungus. The food is manufactured by the alga component, and the fungus provides attachment and a moist environment. Lichens can grow almost anywhere the air is unpolluted, including mountaintops, bare rocks, trees and soil. They grow very slowly, some species less than 1 millimetre in diameter per year, but they can live for several centuries. Since dissimilar organisms cannot reproduce sexually, lichens must reproduce vegetatively, either by airborne dustlike soredia containing cells from both organisms or from fragmentation. Some better-known lichens are the red-topped British soldiers, the old man's beard and the tangled mats of reindeer moss (really a lichen).

Liverworts are either thin, flattened and ribbonlike or leaflike, with two rows of delicate leaves only one cell

Above: British soldiers. Below: Moss.

thick (mosses have spiral leaves). Typical habitats include soil, wet rocks and on wood in a swamp. Markings on some liverworts were thought to resemble the cross section of an animal's liver, hence the name liverwort (liver plant).

Mosses have a characteristic plantlike structure with stem, leaves and fruit. The typical habitat is moist, cool shade, but mosses also grow in the hot, dry environment of exposed rock, depending on the nightly dew for moisture. In contrast, sphagnum moss grows in water and contributes to the transformation of a lake into a habitat suitable for trees. The moss gradually expands to cover the surface of the lake, forming a floating bog and the acidic condition which prevents the decay of vegetation. The accumulation of vegetation over thousands of years fills the lake bed with peat, plant succession takes place, and the forest closes in. The acidic peat has antiseptic qualities and was used for field dressings during the Second World War. Sphagnum moss holds large amounts of water and is effective in preventing flooding and as a moisture retainer in seedbeds.

Identification of mosses, lichens and liverworts presents an interesting challenge for anyone looking for something new. In many cases a stereomicroscope is needed, but with a good 10X hand lens one can become reasonably familiar with the common local species. The guides listed in the references at the back of the book are essential.

Above: Lichens. Below: Club moss.

31

THE HOGS BACK:

On The Ganaraska Trail

Bill Gibbon

One of the favourite walks of Peterborough hikers is over the Hogs Back to Bethany, a portion of the Ganaraska Trail just southwest of the village of Omemee.

This part of the Ganaraska Trail is popular partly because of its proximity to Peterborough, but also because of the views of forests, meadows and hills the path offers along the way. In addition, the 12 kilometres of path give the walker a variety of terrain to traverse, including a few fairly steep hills, on the way to Bethany's ski resorts.

You will find this portion of the trail easily accessible. Proceeding by car along Highway 7 just west of Omemee, turn left at County Road 31 just as the highway bears right and goes up a grade. Continue on this road for nearly 2 kilometres to the second big bend. At this point, a dirt road goes off to the left and down a hill (map ref. N 18). It is suggested that cars be parked at this junction, as driving down the dirt road might damage a car.

Within less than a kilometre, you will come to a concrete bridge that crosses the Pigeon River shortly before it flows into Pigeon Lake north of Omemee. You may want to linger here and enjoy the scenery. In the summertime, you will see water lilies growing in the placid water, swallows diving for insects,

and fishermen trying their luck with lines from the bridge.

The road from the bridge south is little used by vehicles and is certainly not recommended for most cars.

Soon after the bridge, the path begins to climb. It follows an old road that goes up the Hogs Back, an esker formed by a glacier at the end of the Ice Age, 10,000 years ago.

If you follow the road, you will be treading on what is probably the best

example of a glacial deposit in Ontario. The Ministry of Natural Resources has identified it as a "provincially significant area of natural and scientific interest" (ANSI). Consequently, as an aggregate resource, the Hogs Back is protected by the Ministry, and its land use is restricted.

According to local history, the dirt road going over the Hogs Back was a well-used thoroughfare until the railroad, which ran somewhat parallel

Hogs Back

Purple-flowering raspberry

to the old road, was constructed in the mid-1800s.

The ridge at the top of the Hogs Back provides views to the west of lush farmland, cedar-wooded valleys and pointed narrow cones of black spruce, indicating patches of marshy wetlands in the distance. Abandoned farm buildings and split-rail fences along the east side of the trail offer evidence of pioneer farming.

Depending on the season, you can see an abundance of wildflowers, wild strawberries or raspberries along the sides of the path, and wrens and kingbirds in the hedgerows. You may also see hawks searching above the fields for mice. And keep an eye out for the poison ivy that grows along the trail in places.

About 5 kilometres of the path on the Hogs Back is on land owned by a local farmer. The remainder is public road allowance. Keep in mind that the landowner has generously given permission to the Trail Association to allow hikers to cross his land. Show courtesy and respect for private property by staying on the path.

As you are about to come off the Hogs Back, you will come to a branch in the dirt road going downhill to the left. Take the upper road, keep to the right, and check for trail blazes. The trail is fairly well marked with white blazes painted on trees (or on hydro poles in the absence of trees). A single blaze means the path continues on ahead. A set of double blazes indicates the trail makes a turn.

Shortly after the branch in the road, the trail descends through a small woodlot where rotting tree stumps can be seen on either side, silent testimony to the logging of large trees in the area, probably for the building of local farmhouses. At the bottom of this hill, the trail crosses County Road 38 that runs from Omemee to Bethany.

After a short distance on a graded gravel road, the trail continues straight ahead on an earth track while the road branches off to the left. Again, you should check for the white blazes.

After about a kilometre, the trail becomes a gravel road that passes new homes on spacious lots and that leads, after another kilometre, to the Devil's Elbow Ski Resort near Bethany.

Those who wish to start the hike from this end, or wish to place a pick-up car at this end of the trail, should park off the road and outside the ski resort's parking lot. Devil's Elbow is well signed from both Bethany and Omemee along County Road 38.

Other sections of the Ganaraska Trail in the vicinity of Peterborough also offer good walking conditions, with well-marked paths, quiet, no crowds and scenic views.

Altogether, the Ganaraska Hiking Trail extends approximately 400 kilometres from Port Hope to Glen Huron, west of Barrie, where it meets the Bruce Trail. It is maintained by volunteers who are members of one of the association's three clubs in Barrie, Orillia and Peterborough. Guided hikes are sponsored by the clubs in their areas on a weekly basis during spring and fall. A schedule of walks printed in the association's newsletter and a trail guidebook are available with the payment of a membership fee.

32

A LOOP TRAIL FROM BETHANY

Gordon Berry

This 7-kilometre walk covers some of the prettiest countryside in the area. It offers tremendous views of distant farms nestling in shallow valleys among fields snipped from a patchwork of wooded hills, all loosely stitched together with threads of highway.

The walk starts from Roberts Street, beside the Bethany Post Office on Highway 7A (map ref. M 18). While Roberts Street boasts a name and a sign, the street is paved for only 100 metres and then immediately dwindles into a stony track. The trail climbs among some gnarled and twisted trees, and around some burned-out farm buildings, before expanding onto a landscape of sandy hills and fine open country.

The soil here is soft sand and appears to have no humus content at all. The hills are covered with a meagre blanket of coarse grasses that struggle to keep a foothold in this impoverished soil. The land has been deforested at some time in the past, probably by homesteaders who did not understand the perilous consequences of their action. With the tree cover gone, the thin topsoil was quickly eroded and lost. In recent years some extensive replanting has been carried out to remedy this condition. These areas can be seen on the left as you follow the trail. The young spruce and pine trees now help to hold the soil, and a mat of good ground cover is developing among them.

On the right, the gentle rolling hills are lightly peppered with a few large rocks and the occasional erratic boulder. The land here is struggling against the activity of motorbikes and all-terrain vehicles. These vehicles have destroyed the thin surface cover of grass; the sand is exposed and considerable erosion is taking place.

From the top of the rise there are magnificent views on both sides. Linger and enjoy the wide panorama which stretches away in hazy blues to the distant horizon.

The trail soon splits, with a wheeled track branching to the left, while another track leads on through a small quarry where sand and gravel have been excavated. On the other side of the depression the trail splits again, a single path leading ahead and a grassy

Hepatica

Woodland walk

two-wheeled track branching to the left. All these trails lead to the same place, so it does not matter which you take. I prefer the grassy, wider trail which passes through the reforested fields, as it is less sandy and easier to walk.

In summer, the new growth beneath the small trees is embroidered with meadow wildflowers and flowers common to disturbed soil: the bright orange and yellow hawkweeds, fleabanes and daisies.

Where the tracks meet again, at the end of the reforested area, there is a well-defined dirt roadway which crosses at right angles. Beyond is a small stand of Scotch pine. Note this junction well, as you will return to this point at the end of the looped trail. Across the roadway and a few metres to the right, a rough path leads in among the pines.

These tall pines are about 35 years old and have recently been selectively cut. The branches and debris have been left in piles to provide shelter for ruffed grouse and other woodland creatures and to avoid repeating the mistakes of former tree harvesters.

High above the trail, the pines seem to gossip a whispered commentary about our progress as they sway gently to a breezy bidding. Red squirrels rattle away, protesting the walkers' invasion of their domain, and the smudged tracks of raccoons, rabbits and squirrels can be seen in the sandy path.

On the other side of this stand of pines, along the upper boundary, a grassy path bears to the left. After a short distance the path crosses a cut wire fence, then turns to the right again. (Be careful, the wires are on the ground and difficult to see.)

A pleasant contrast is now offered the walker. Open fields replace the sandy hills on one side, while the path gently descends through open climax woods of maple, elm and birch. In these sheltered areas, where enough trees have been left to protect the land, a rich leafy loam has accumulated, and this provides a habitat for trilliums, bellwort, columbine, hepatica, adder's tongue and other spring flowers.

The trail now meets another well-used trail at a T junction; turn left here. Further evidence of erosion from poor land management can be seen on the left. The stumps of trees cut in years gone by are scattered across the sandy slopes and stand like gravestones, testimony to man's folly and the passing of something loved and beautiful.

Eventually the trail leads to a gravelled road. A little to the left, on a small tree on the opposite side of the road, is the white blaze mark of the Ganaraska Trail Association. Turn left onto the roadway and follow the road for about 1 kilometre. This small county road has the unusual distinction of having a name rather than a number: Dranoel Road (Leonard spelled backwards).

Follow this road until you come to an abandoned railway bed which crosses the road diagonally. Turn left onto the gravel bed of this forgotten railway and after 200 metres you will come to another rough track that crosses at right angles. Here you have a choice. You can follow the old railway bed right back to the Bethany Post Office, or you can turn left and this earth road will lead you back to the junction near the stand of pines that was mentioned earlier. From there you can retrace your steps across the open sandy hills back to the start.

33

THE GANARASKA FOREST

James Tedford, Ganaraska Region Conservation Authority

There is more to the Ganaraska Forest than 4,455 hectares of trees, trails, wildlife and flowers. The Ganaraska Forest has a history. It controls flooding and stops erosion, it is a source of wood for the logging industry, and it provides a rich educational opportunity for children to study the environment. Venture south on Highway 28 to Rice Lake, then turn west onto County Road 9 to experience the wonder of the Ganaraska Forest (map ref. M 17). The Ganaraska Forest Centre is signed on the right-hand side of the highway.

The Ganaraska Forest area has seen many changes. Two hundred years ago the trees of this area provided the tall masts for the sailing ships of the British Navy. One hundred years ago it was covered with productive farmland. Fifty years ago the land lay barren, a landscape of dunes and blowing sand. Today it is re-established as a forest with many uses.

The forest was created for two reasons, to reduce flooding in Port Hope and to stabilize the soils along this section of the Oak Ridges Moraine. Both objectives have been achieved, and the forest represents one of the most successful conservation measures ever undertaken in Ontario.

The history of man's activity on the moraine, until recent years, has largely been a history of mistakes and ignorance of good land management practices. When vegetation is totally removed from fine, sandy soils such as are found along the moraine, soil loss almost inevitably occurs. Early lumbermen and pioneer farmers did not have the experience and knowledge we have today. (However, these same practices are producing the same results in the Queen Charlotte Islands in British Columbia, in parts of northern Ontario, and in the rain forests of Brazil.)

The Ganaraska Forest stretches from Highway 28 in the east to Highway 115/35 in the west. Driving through the forest on one of the 150 kilometres of roads you might get the impression that most of the forest is plantation. Although over 5 million trees have been planted, they account for only half of the forest. The other half is natural, containing maple, oak, cherry, hemlock, birch and many other species. Stream valleys are predominantly cedar. The main species planted is red pine; however, white pine, white spruce and larch have also been planted.

Today, the Ganaraska Forest produces wood for log homes, hydro poles, lumber and firewood, as well as for paper and related products. The forest is home to a wide variety of recreational activities, but unfortunately not all of these activities are compatible. Inevitably conflicts arise between motorized and non-motorized users. The Ganaraska Region Conservation Authority has formed a committee composed of user group representatives who have established guidelines for the recreational use of the forest.

To help reduce these conflicts, the Ganaraska Forest is divided into three

Wild turkey

Ganaraska Forest Centre Trails

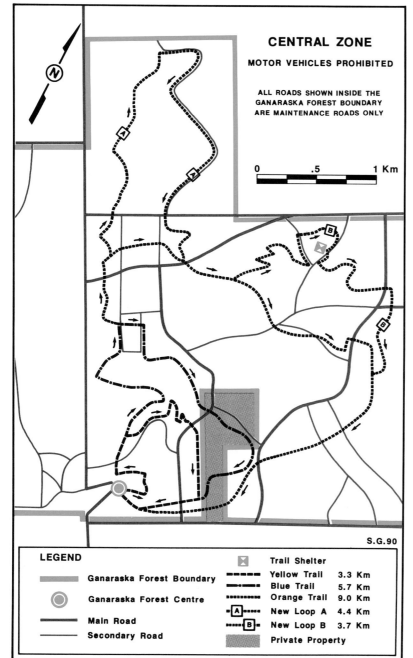

CENTRAL ZONE

MOTOR VEHICLES PROHIBITED

ALL ROADS SHOWN INSIDE THE
GANARASKA FOREST BOUNDARY
ARE MAINTENANCE ROADS ONLY

0   .5   1 Km

S.G.90

LEGEND

▨	Trail Shelter	
Ganaraska Forest Boundary	Yellow Trail	3.3 Km
	Blue Trail	5.7 Km
◉ Ganaraska Forest Centre	Orange Trail	9.0 Km
	Ⓐ New Loop A	4.4 Km
Main Road	Ⓑ New Loop B	3.7 Km
Secondary Road	Private Property	

Wild turkeys were introduced into the forest in 1988. These birds can weigh up to 10 kilograms. During the winter, the turkeys can be found in the forest, where they feed on nuts, seeds, grass and weeds. In the spring, summer and fall, the turkeys can be found in pasture and field areas and along the edge between field and forest. Insects and waste grain are important food sources. A wide variety of other birds and animals can be seen on your visit to the Ganaraska Forest.

All trails in the Ganaraska Forest are accessible from the Forest Centre. Thirty kilometres of trail for cross-country skiing and hiking originate from this area and extend for up to 16 kilometres into the non-motorized use area. A short interpretive trail begins at the centre as well. This trail will provide you with an introduction to the history of the area and will show you some of the forest management practices being carried out.

For those of you who are more energetic, the orange trail will take you on a 16-kilometre hike from the Forest Centre through a variety of terrain and forest types. In the winter, these trails are groomed and track-set for skiing. The 30 kilometres of ski trails available offer a challenge for even the most accomplished skier. Other trails are available for motorcycle and snowmobile use.

As well as being the starting point for trails, the Forest Centre is also the site of the Conservation Authority's conservation education program. Under this program, students from Port Hope, Peterborough, Oshawa and the surrounding areas live at the Forest Centre for 2 1/2 days, learning about the environment and their role in it.

different use zones. The east and west zones are designated for both motorized and non-motorized activities. Hunting is also allowed in these areas under municipal and provincial regulations. The central zone is reserved for non-motorized activities, with hunting being confined to a small area.

100

White pine

Red pine

White spruce

Ganaraska Forest

Top row, left to right: Arethusa, White-fringed orchis, Pink lady's-slipper. Bottom row, left to right: Ram's head lady's-slipper, Grass pink.

34

ORCHIDS OF THE KAWARTHAS

Gordon Berry

It may come as a surprise to some people to learn that there are orchids in the Peterborough area. The term "orchid" is often associated with rare exotic blooms found in greenhouses or tropical forests rather than in our locality. Certainly there are more species of these fragile flowers in the rain forests of Southeast Asia and the Amazon, but you can sometimes find an occasional orchid in your lawn! Helleborine, an aggressive invader from Europe which is often considered a weed by gardeners, shows up in grassy areas, flower beds and roadside margins in Peterborough and other areas.

Orchids are possibly the largest of all the families of flowering plants, with some 20,000 known species. They have adapted to a wide range of habitat, from epiphytic species (plants that grow on other species) that are found in tropical trees to terrestrial forms found in moist woodlots and swamps. A few, such as the coral-roots, lack chlorophyll and depend on decaying vegetable matter for their energy.

Orchids are most easily recognized by their flowers, and while these vary enormously in size, form, colour and fragrance, they all have a few characteristics in common. Orchids have three sepals which often resemble petals. There are three petals with the centre one usually larger and of a different shape than the other two. As the part of the stem that holds the ovary often bends forward through 180 degrees, this larger petal, the labellum, projects forward and downward at the base of the flower. This structure may act as a landing platform for pollinators. The sexual parts, which produce or receive pollen and contain the ova, vary widely in shape and specialization. The sexual or seed-producing parts of other flowers (the stamen and the pistil) are separate, but in orchids these parts are fused into many different forms, unique to each species. All orchids are perennials with rhizomes or tuberous roots.

Orchids have developed a very special relationship with insects and probably show the greatest specialization for pollination of any family of plants, having unique odours and bizarre structures to attract insects. Many orchids limit their pollinators to just one or at most a very few species of insect. At least one variety uses the activities of the mosquito as a pollinator! Charles Darwin was so fascinated by the adaptions of these plants that he wrote an entire book on the subject. The book proved extremely popular and stimulated all kinds of new research.

The best-known Ontario orchids are the lady's-slipper varieties, with the characteristic slipper shape of their large labellum. The yellow lady's-slipper grows in rich open maple and beech woodland. The stemless lady's-slipper, or moccasin flower, displays colourful rose-veined petals. The lower "shoe" petal is partly divided and looks rather like a pair of ballet slippers hung up by their heels. The showy lady's-slipper is the largest and most strikingly coloured flower, boasting white petals and a rose-tinted centre, while the dainty ram's head orchid, which is now quite rare, is found among cedar roots in swampy areas and in open mixed woods.

One of the most dramatic and beautiful orchids found in the Kawarthas, the arethusa, or dragon-mouth orchid, has a delicate pink flower with a yellow pollen-furred tongue. It is found in sphagnum moss among the long grasses in bogs and fens. This orchid is also becoming very difficult to find. Rose pogonia or grass pinks are very similar to the arethusa, both in colour and form, and are often present as a companion species.

There are probably between 35 and 40 species of orchids to be found in the Kawarthas. Other orchids that have been seen in this area include nodding ladies' tresses, hooded ladies' tresses, showy orchis, striped coral-root, and the tessellated rattlesnake plantain.

It may seem strange that in a book such as this there is no specific

indication of where these colourful orchids are to be found. Unfortunately, many species of orchid are now quite rare and almost every species needs protection. About one third of the 60 species of orchids found in Ontario are now classified as either rare or uncommon. The natural habitat of many species, such as bogs and other wetlands, are under constant pressure from development projects of all kinds. The very beauty of these plants makes them prey to thoughtless persons who may pick them. I once saw two large buckets of stemless lady's-slippers for sale in the Peterborough market on Decoration Day! It is perhaps fortunate that their best protection is the fact that many of them bloom when the black-flies and mosquitoes are most voracious and few

people venture into swampy areas in spring. They are also tempting prizes for those who want to dig them up and transplant them to their own gardens. Such transplants are almost never successful. Gardens can rarely provide the type of soil, proper acidity, moisture, shade and pollinators which these plants need. This is true for most wildflowers. To move flowers from their natural habitat almost certainly means that they will die within a year, that they will not regenerate as might be expected if they were left to flower, and it may well be that a rare species is hurried toward extinction.

The Cavan Swamp, which covers some 1,011 hectares, is one of the richest sites for orchids in Ontario. Some 194 hectares of this swamp have been

Yellow lady's-slipper

purchased by the Otonabee Region Conservation Authority, with the help of the Nature Conservancy of Canada, to preserve and protect this fragile and sensitive area. There are no footpaths through the swamp to the areas where the orchids are found, and most species occur in small numbers and are hard to find. The Conservation Authority cannot protect these plants and at the same time encourage people to visit the swamp. It is unfortunate that these beautiful flowers must be protected in this way, but our generation, which has destroyed so many species of plants and animals, must take the responsibility for protecting and saving what we can.

35

GARDEN HILL CONSERVATION AREA

James Tedford, Ganaraska Region Conservation Authority

Garden Hill Conservation Area is located on County Road 9 just west of Highway 28 (map ref. M 17). This area boasts a 14-hectare pond with an adjoining picnic area, which makes it especially popular on hot summer days. In the early spring and fall, migrating waterfowl use the pond as a staging area before flying further north or south. Thousands of ducks and geese can be found on the pond during this time of year. Fishing is also popular. Put your canoe into the pond and fish for the elusive brown or speckled trout. Please, no motorized craft are permitted on the pond.

Several pleasant, but unsigned, walking trails can be reached by taking the gravel road that runs along the west side of the Garden Hill property. Follow this road for about 1 kilometre and it ends in a T junction. Take the left-hand track and explore the wooded areas along the fringes of the Ganaraska Forest.

Access to the Ganaraska Hiking Trail can also be found on these trails; watch for the white blaze marks. A short loop trail within the Conservation Area allows for a pleasant afternoon stroll through the woods.

A cairn at the entrance to the Conservation Area commemorates the Guelph Conference of 1941. Recommendations from this conference led to the creation of the Conservation Authorities of Ontario.

Canada geese

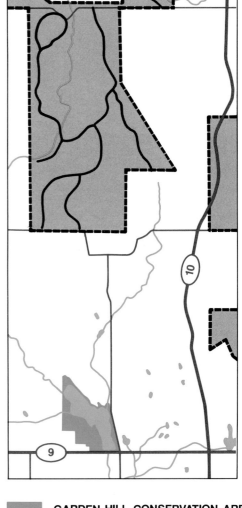

GARDEN HILL CONSERVATION AREA

GANARASKA FOREST

TRAIL

Porcupine

Red squirrel

Chipmunk

Deer mouse

36

MAMMALS

Geoffrey Carpentier

Peterborough County is divided by a rocky granite outcrop known as the Precambrian Shield. Areas to the north are typified by deep, rocky lakes, bogs, extensive poplar and hemlock groves, and scattered small agricultural communities. South of the Shield, agricultural and urban development predominates. However, extensive remnant forests, fence rows, overgrown fields, marshes and bogs still persist. This combination of almost every type of habitat has given the county an inordinately high diversity of species for this part of the province. Sixty species of mammals representing 16 families have been recorded. As might be expected, the various types of habitat support different species of animals in the north and in the south.

Animals have long roamed our land, but glaciation and a variety of man-induced pressures, including land clearing and hunting, have greatly restricted or enhanced specific mammalian populations.

Species such as the lynx, wolverine, caribou and elk are likely gone from this area forever. Others, such as the pine marten and grey fox, persist in extremely low, non-sustaining numbers. Cougars and badgers have been sighted recently, but their source and the reason for their return remains obscure. Timber wolves, moose, otters and the like still roam the northern reaches,

while groundhogs, deer and grey squirrels predominate in the south.

Northern populations are presumably little changed from historic times, as the habitat has remained relatively undisturbed. Perhaps only the beaver and white-tailed deer are now more abundant, as game management practices have positively affected their populations. The other furbearers, with the exception of lynx, marten and fisher, are probably present in numbers similar to those our ancestors saw.

More easily understood are the opportunistic species that do so well in disturbed habitats. Any animal that can learn to tolerate man will have an edge in the game of survival; for example, the raccoon and the chipmunk.

Conditions in the south are conducive to the expansion of the irruptive species. Expanding and invading species are generally the most adaptive, as they are able to take advantage of emerging, expanding or enhanced habitats. Animals that are intolerant of disturbance rarely

Groundhog

Black bear

Hare

survive. The characteristics of the successful species must include a high birth rate, low infant mortality, varied and adaptive diets, and tolerance of man. Squirrels steal our birdseed, live in our attics and sometimes become family pets. Raccoons share our homes and garbage. Coyotes interbreed with dogs to produce coydogs. Groundhogs live in farmers' fields and our gardens. Bats live in our attics with the family treasures, and deer feed in our orchards.

One would expect that the trust or complacency these animals exhibit towards man would make them easy targets for control. On the contrary, these animals persist and, in fact, their populations expand annually.

Interestingly, Peterborough represents the southern or northern range limit of several species of mammals. Included in the former group are the northern flying squirrels, moose, timber wolf and pine marten. Representatives of the latter group include the white-footed mouse, southern flying squirrel and grey fox.

Finding mammals in an area as large and diverse as Peterborough County takes a little practice, but with patience, the task can be most rewarding. Searching for mammals is made more difficult due to several factors. Mammals are generally non-social, avoid human contact, are nocturnal and often occupy inaccessible or difficult terrain. However, outings can be quite successful if a few simple rules are followed.

First, one must attain a reasonable knowledge of the preferred habitat, behaviour and habits of the species sought. It makes little sense to search for moose in the urbanized parts of the county! Questions should be posed in advance. What does the animal look like? Does it live in the woods, fields or marshlands? What does it eat? What kind of tracks or signs does it leave? Does it produce any vocalizations? Is it active by day or night? Does it hibernate?

With a good understanding of the animal, one can proceed to the field in search of the species. Field work can be surprisingly easy with some species. Squirrels, groundhogs, skunks, rabbits and deer are often highly visible because of their gregarious behaviour and tolerance of man. In fact, most prey species are more readily observed than predators, simply because they are more numerous.

To discover the rarer animals, a few hints on location and habits may be helpful. Talk to the locals about wolf packs or fox dens, read the newspapers for interesting sightings, but foremost, be patient. Drive the back roads at dusk or, better still, at dawn. Choose a spot in an area well used by mammals and wait quietly. Watch for evidence of feces, tracks in the mud or snow, twigs that have been torn or chewed off bushes, shredded bark, scent posts, fur on bushes, or the remains of kills. All will offer good clues to the presence of a species. Many predators become somewhat vocal and more active in late winter and early spring as the reproductive season heightens. Finally, watch along the roadways for animals killed by cars. These will give good indications of what is around and possibly their abundance. Combining all these factors will almost guarantee some interesting wildlife encounters.

There are several good sources of information available to individuals interested in searching for mammals. The Peterborough Field Naturalists, Ministry of Natural Resources, Trent University and Sir Sandford Fleming College all have qualified individuals familiar with local populations. Additionally, some of these same groups have stuffed specimens available for study.

37

SERPENT MOUNDS PROVINCIAL PARK

Mandy Bidwell, Ministry of Natural Resources

Nestled among the rolling hills of the Peterborough Drumlin Fields, overlooking scenic Rice Lake, lies Serpent Mounds Provincial Park, the hidden jewel of the Kawarthas (map ref. M 16).

For generations, visitors have been drawn to this idyllic setting where you can camp or picnic beneath shade trees; swim, boat and fish in the warm waters of Rice Lake; or just sit atop a drumlin prominence and appreciate what nature has to offer.

Transcending even the aesthetic appeal of the park is the greater realization that this area figured so prominently in the prehistory of Canada.

Over 2,000 years ago, the native people belonging to the Point Peninsula Culture began to gather on this point of land. Each spring and summer, families would camp here and gather shellfish and wild rice from the shallows of the lake. Centuries have passed since the Point Peninsula People last visited this spot, yet beneath the soil their legacy remains.

Situated among a grove of aging oaks, on a knoll above Rice Lake, are nine burial mounds which cover the remains of these people of the past. Eight of the burial mounds have a simple oval design, while the ninth and largest mound forms a serpentine shape, hence "Serpent Mound" from which the park derived its name.

The serpentine-shaped mound, the only one of its kind in Canada, measures 59 metres in length, averages about 8 metres in width, and varies up to 2 metres in height!

In the late 1950s an extensive archaeological dig was conducted by researchers from the Royal Ontario Museum. It has been estimated that construction of the "serpent mound" possibly began around A.D. 128, with the final graves being added some 200 years later!

These burial mounds symbolized a deep concern for the dead and the afterlife. Many grave goods, such as shells, flint projectile points, fossils, copper and silver beads, mammal bones and bone harpoons, were uncovered. It is believed that these objects were of sentimental value and were placed in the grave so that they would accompany the spirit of the dead.

Further evidence of the mound builders' lifestyle was revealed in a shoreline habitation area and a shell refuse heap, commonly referred to as the midden. The midden was quite extensive, measuring 90 x 10 metres, and consisted mainly of thick layers of broken clam shells and fragments of clay pottery. The abundance of clam shells indicated that the mound builders came to this area in the spring and summer, since the lake would have been frozen and the clams unattainable in the winter. The distinct impressions which decorated the pottery pieces helped identify these early habitants as a Point Peninsula band.

Many changes have transpired since the mound builders first camped on the shores of Rice Lake, but their memory lives on. In order to preserve and protect the natural and cultural heritage of the area, Serpent Mounds Provincial Park was established.

Today, an interpretive trail, with illustrated panels describing the Point Peninsula People and their summer camps, winds past the burial mounds to the Visitor Centre. The Visitor Centre contains native artifacts and displays which depict the lifestyle of the mound builders. A natural environment theme is also present, with special emphasis on the extensive wetland complex on Harris Island, located southeast of the park mainland.

Also part of the park, Harris Island has been designated as a provincially significant area of scientific and natural interest (ANSI) which provides representation of two features, a marsh and drumlin island complex. This island has been selected as one of the few undisturbed forested drumlin islands in the Peterborough Drumlin Fields.

The island wetlands attract large numbers of resident and migrational flocks of ducks, bitterns, herons and songbirds, as well as mammals such as muskrat and beaver.

Rice Lake is the largest lake in the area and one of Ontario's most important warm-water sport fisheries. The shallowness of the lake, in conjunction with sunlight, promotes a tremendous growth rate among weeds, a condition which enhances the fish population. The protected waters of Harris Island house a variety of sport fish, including smallmouth and largemouth bass, muskellunge and walleye (pickerel), as well as a variety of panfish, including sunfish, perch and rock bass.

Serpent Mounds Provincial Park continues to be a popular camping spot and attracts fishermen, sunbathers, historical buffs and tour groups to its tranquil, scenic shores.

Serpent mound

38

PETER'S WOODS PROVINCIAL NATURE RESERVE

Mandy Bidwell, Ministry of Natural Resources

Imagine yourself as one of the first settlers to arrive in southern Ontario. Imagine being greeted by magnificent stands of white pine, oak, maple and beech. Today, only vestiges of these towering giants remain.

Peter's Woods Provincial Nature Reserve offers refuge to these stalwart survivors. Nature Reserve provincial parks represent the distinctive natural habitats and landforms of the province. These areas of land are protected for educational purposes and research which will benefit present and future generations.

In order to preserve and perpetuate, in a relatively natural condition, a remnant stand of the mature forest that once covered large portions of southern Ontario, Peter's Woods Provincial Nature Reserve was established. The reserve is on lots 14 and 15 of Concession 8 of Haldimand Township (map ref. M 16). Travel east from Highway 45 on County Road 29 to the second road on the right and go 2 kilometres south to the reserve. (If you get to Burnley, you have gone too far!)

The acquisition of this land was the result of co-operative efforts between the Willow Beach Field Naturalists and the Ontario Ministry of Natural Resources. Peter's Woods is named in honour of Mr. A.B. "Peter" Schultz, a naturalist, conservationist and leading member of the Willow Beach Field Naturalists.

The topography of this 33-hectare Nature Reserve was determined over 12,000 years ago, during the last ice age. Massive glaciers scraped and pushed bedrock and soils to form what is referred to as the Oak Ridges Moraine. In the Peterborough area these glaciers created the Peterborough Drumlin Fields, hundreds of long, streamlined hills, steep at one end and tapered at the other, which point in the direction the glacier flowed. Peter's Woods virtually straddles the boundary between the Oak Ridges Moraine and the Peterborough Drumlin Fields.

A 0.8-kilometre loop walking trail through the rolling landscape of Peter's Woods offers you a glimpse into Ontario's past. The trail begins by passing through an abandoned farm field where early stages of succession are evident. Shade-tolerant species such as white pine and maple are quickly dominating the sun-loving trees and

Fungus

Chipmunk

shrubs. This forces less shade-tolerant species such as basswood, choke cherry and ash to move forward into the sunny open field.

Leaving behind the battle for succession and grassy fields of goldenrod, ragweed and saplings, the trail circles down and crosses an intermittent stream to a mature beech-maple community. An extremely shade-tolerant species, beech requires plenty of cover and rich soils. When settling this part of the province, early pioneers often looked for the presence of beech as an indicator of good farmland. The virginal beech forests were cleared for agriculture, and second-generation beech growth is now flourishing.

Off in the distance is the unmistakable silhouette of Ontario's provincial tree, the white pine. While walking among these immense trees, some with trunks more than a metre across, you experience a sense of the forests of two centuries ago. Gazing up at the tall, straight trunks of the white pine, it is easy to imagine why these noble trees were once popular as ship masts for the Royal Navy. Although nearly all of Ontario's white pine of this size has been removed, we are fortunate to have these fine samples in Peter's Woods.

Continuing along the trail, the boulders of the Oak Ridges Moraine become more evident, and the soil becomes poorer and thinner. Lacking a rich, fertile environment, the previously dominant white pine, maple and beech grow much less vigorously here. This lack of competition promotes the growth of yellow birch, a species which adapts well to moderate shade conditions where the leaf layer is sparse enough to allow their weak roots to penetrate. The shallow, rocky soil of the Oak Ridges Moraine provides an excellent habitat for yellow birch.

Once again crossing the intermittent stream which flows through Peter's Woods, the trail passes by a low-lying wetland area where white cedar and balsam fir dominate. Wetland areas are capable of supporting a higher concentration of life than any other habitat type. Fish, birds, mammals, amphibians, reptiles, bacteria, fungi and invertebrates can all exist within a wetland. This sensitive area is fragile and visitors are asked not to stray off the marked path!

The trail continues up and along the top of the ravine, and loops back to the parking lot.

Peter's Woods Provincial Nature Reserve lies in a region marked by its diversity of vegetation, ranging from open fields to mature deciduous woods, to coniferous forests, and to sensitive marsh areas. In addition, a rich ground flora supports a wealth of wildflowers such as red and white trilliums, spotted touch-me-not, wild lily of the valley and purple asters.

This extensive variety of vegetation provides a variety of mammals and birds with a wide range of habitats. You are encouraged to take advantage of the rest stops along the trail. By quietly letting your senses absorb the surrounding environment, you may witness the antics of a red squirrel, imitate the call of a song sparrow, lazily observe the hypnotic soaring of a red-tailed hawk, smell the freshness of wild spring flowers, ponder the tracks of a white-tailed deer — experience the wonders of Peter's Woods Provincial Nature Reserve.

The objective of the reserve is to protect the stand of mature forests, cedar swamp wetland and adjacent field habitats by allowing change to take place as a natural process. When the trail was being constructed, care was taken not to remove or disrupt the vegetation. Visitors are asked to please restrict all walks and exploration to the trail itself. The wet soils, spring banks and delicate plants are easily damaged. A self-guiding trail brochure is available at the trail entrance.

Winter use in the Nature Reserve is limited, as no services are provided and park gates are kept closed. Visitors may enter for snowshoeing and cross-country skiing.

39

TRACKS IN THE SNOW

Clay Vardy

Many animals, being nocturnal or very shy, are difficult to see. A great deal of patient waiting and watching is required. However, in winter, they leave a readily visible record of their presence through their tracks. Not only do tracks give us an indication of what animal has passed by, but they can also tell us something of the animal's habits.

Ideal conditions for reading tracks are 2 to 3 centimetres of fresh or wet snow. Tracks can also be seen in mud and wet sand along stream banks.

The following are some of the more common tracks to be found in the Peterborough area.

See illustration on page 114.

Deer Mouse, Meadow Vole and Shrew

Small, dainty tracks, often with a line caused by the tail dragging, will belong to a deer mouse, meadow vole or one of the shrews. The deer mouse tends to bound (hind feet landing first), whereas the others often change from bounding to running or walking even over a short distance. All of them tend to move in random circular patterns with frequent burrowing into the snow.

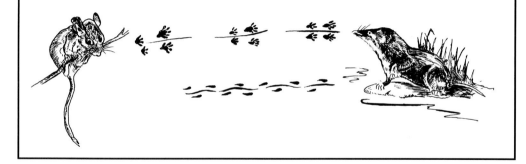

Squirrels

Squirrel tracks typically can be traced from tree to tree. By following squirrel tracks, holes in the snow surrounded by seed shells can be found. These are the sites of seed caches made during the fall for winter use.

Squirrels often leave a distinctive smudged rectangular print in the snow as they travel close to the ground and their paws drag across the surface of the snow.

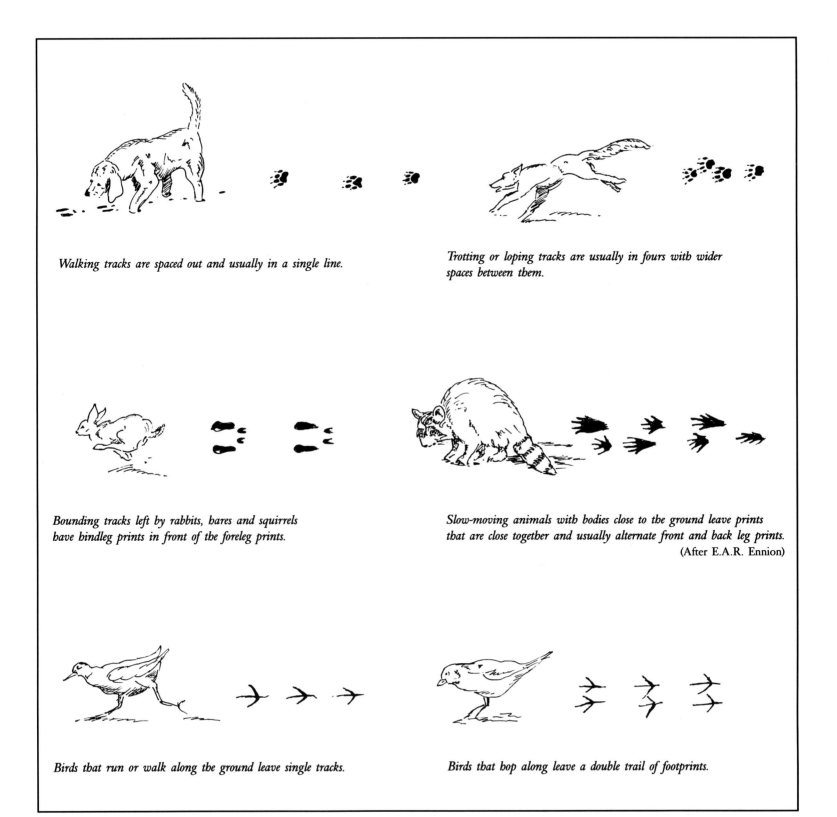

Walking tracks are spaced out and usually in a single line.

Trotting or loping tracks are usually in fours with wider spaces between them.

Bounding tracks left by rabbits, hares and squirrels have hindleg prints in front of the foreleg prints.

Slow-moving animals with bodies close to the ground leave prints that are close together and usually alternate front and back leg prints.

(After E.A.R. Ennion)

Birds that run or walk along the ground leave single tracks.

Birds that bop along leave a double trail of footprints.

Cottontail Rabbit / Snowshoe Hare

Rabbit and hare tracks are unmistakable, with large hind feet landing in front of their small forefeet during typical hopping motion. Hare are much larger than rabbits and a clear footprint in the snow shows how aptly named are "snowshoe" hare. Hare can move extremely quickly and leap an incredible distance when necessary.

Raccoon

The raccoon generally has a slow, ambling gait, placing the hind foot beside the forefoot. The prints often show well-defined fingers and toes, with the hind foot being much larger than the fore.

Deer

Deer prints are distinctive, being the only wild hoofed animal in our area. Having relatively small, pointed feet, deer tend to sink into deep snow, often leaving deep, ill-defined prints. Because of this penetration, they often follow the harder, packed snow of snowmobile or ski trails. Here, their distinctive hoof marks may be more clearly seen. When they are walking, their fore and hind feet make prints that almost overlap. When they are travelling fast, the prints are deeper and are spread out into groups of four.

Red Fox

One of the most beautiful sights in winter is the slowly meandering, dainty set of prints made by a fox crossing newly fallen snow. When the fox is walking, the prints fall almost one behind the other in a straight line. As with all canine species the claw marks are usually visible. When foxes are travelling fast they bound along, leaving groups of four prints with large distances between each group.

It can be difficult to distinguish between the various canine species.

Each of these animals has a similar paw print, with pads and claws well defined. Generally, domestic dogs do not place their paws one behind the other as the fox does, but have a wider straddle. As there are so many breeds of dogs, from large to small, size is of little help in distinguishing their tracks from fox or wolf. Dogs seem to wander all over the territory beside the trail as they usually stay close to the people they accompany. As they are not aware of a need for protection, they make no use of available cover.

Wolves (not common in the Peterborough area, but several packs known in the Crown Game Preserve) have larger prints than most dogs, up to 11 centimetres long, and they make good use of cover.

The coyote's prints are only slightly larger than the fox's but they do not fall in such a straight line.

Grouse

Sometimes a clear line of crosses can be seen in the snow, especially in clearings in the woods. These belong to the ruffed grouse. They clearly show the three large toes and small fourth hind toe. In the Ganaraska Forest similar but larger tracks may be made by the wild turkeys that have been released there.

Grouse often shelter from the wind and cold by burying themselves in soft snow. Occasionally, when walking or skiing in the woods, you may see one of these birds spring explosively from the snow, leaving a hole and a wonderful impression of its spread wings on the surface, a nearly perfect "angel."

The next time that you are out walking or cross-country skiing and you see tracks in the snow, take a few minutes to study them. Maybe you will learn a little about the animal that made them. What was it? Which way was it going? Was it looking for food? What food? Was it being chased by a predator? Tracks in the snow are a great way to add to our enjoyment of our winter environment.

REFERENCE LIST

ANIMALS

Borror, Donald J., and Richard E. White. *A Field Guide to the Insects.* Boston: Houghton Mifflin Company, 1974.

Brewer, J., and Dave Winter. *Butterflies and Moths: A Companion to Your Field Guide.* New York: Prentice Hall Press, 1986.

Carpentier, Geoffrey. *The Mammals of Peterborough County.* Peterborough: Orchid Press, 1987.

Conant, Roger. *A Field Guide to Reptiles and Amphibians of Eastern and Central North America.* Boston: Houghton Mifflin Company, 1975.

Fenton, M. Brock. *Just Bats.* Toronto: University of Toronto Press, 1983.

Klots, Alexander B. *A Field Guide to the Butterflies of Eastern North America.* Boston: Houghton Mifflin Company, 1976.

Murie, Olaus J. *A Field Guide to Animal Tracks.* Boston: Houghton Mifflin Company, 1974.

Zim, Herbert S., and Clarence Cottam. *Insects.* New York: Golden Press, Western Publishing Company, 1987.

Pyle, Robert M. *The Audubon Society Field Guide to North American Butterflies.* New York: Alfred A. Knopf, 1981.

Pyle, Robert M. *The Audubon Society Handbook for Butterfly Watchers.* New York: Scribner's Sons, 1984.

BIRDS

Peterson, Roger Tory. *A Field Guide to the Birds East of the Rockies.* Boston: Houghton Mifflin Company, 1984.

Sadler, Doug. *Our Heritage of Birds.* Peterborough: Orchid Press, 1983.

Scott, Shirley L. *National Geographic Society Field Guide to the Birds of North America.* Washington: National Geographic Society, 1983.

GEOLOGY and GEOMORPHOLOGY

Adams, Peter, and Colin Taylor. *Peterborough and the Kawarthas.* Peterborough: Heritage Publications, 1987.

Brunger, Alan. *By Lake and Lock.* Peterborough: Heritage Peterborough, 1987.

Hewitt, D.F. *Geology and Scenery, Peterborough, Bancroft and Madoc Area.* Ontario Dept. Mines, Geol. Guide Book 3, 1969 (reprinted, currently out of print).

Mallory, Enid. *KAWARTHA: Living on These Lakes.* Peterborough Publishing, 1991.

Sabina, Ann P. *Rocks and Minerals for the Collector, Hull-Maniwaki, Quebec; Ottawa-Peterborough, Ontario.* Ottawa: Geological Survey of Canada, 1980.

PLANTS

Brodo, Irwin M. *Lichens of the Ottawa Region.* Ottawa: National Museum of Natural Sciences, 1988.

Cody, William J., and Donald M. Britton. *Ferns and Fern Allies of Canada.* Ottawa: Agriculture Canada, 1989.

Conrad, Henry S., and Paul L. Redfern, Jr. *How to Know the Mosses and Liverworts.* Dubuque, Iowa: Wm. C. Brown Company, 1986 (out of print).

Groves, J. Walton. *Edible and Poisonous Mushrooms of Canada.* Ottawa: Agriculture Canada, 1979.

Hale, Mason E. *How to Know the Lichens.* Dubuque, Iowa: Wm.C. Brown Company, 1979.

Hosie, R.C. *Native Trees of Canada.* Ottawa: Canadian Forestry Service, 1990.

Lauriault, J. *Identification Guide to the Trees of Canada.* Markham: Fitzhenry and Whiteside, 1989.

Alex, J.F., and C.M. Switzer. *Ontario Weeds.* Toronto: Ontario Department of Agriculture and Food, No. 505, 1976.

Newcomb, Lawrence. *Newcomb's Wildflower Guide.* Toronto: Little, Brown and Company, 1989.

Rose, A.H., and O.H. Lindquist. *Insects of Eastern Hardwood Trees.* Ottawa: Ministry of Supply and Services, 1982.

Soper, James H., and Margaret L. Heimburger. *Shrubs of Ontario.* Toronto: The Royal Ontario Museum, 1985.

White, J.H., and R.C. Hosie. *The Forest Trees of Ontario.* Toronto: Ministry of Natural Resources, 1990.

SKY

Canada, Ministry of Supply and Services. *Learning Weather: A Resource Study Kit.* Ottawa: Canadian Government Publishing Centre, 1989.

Dickson, Terence. *Nightwatch, an Equinox Guide to Viewing the Universe.* Camden East: Camden House Publishing Ltd., 1989.

SOURCES OF INFORMATION

Federation of Ontario Naturalists,
355 Lesmill Road,
Don Mills, Ontario,
M3B 2W8   416-444-8419

Ministry of Natural Resources:

1. District Office:
   P.O. Box 500, Bancroft, Ontario,
   K0L 1C0   613-332-3940
   Silent Lake: 613-339-2807
   Petroglyphs: 705-877-2552

2. District Office:
   332 Kent St. West, Lindsay, Ontario,
   K9V 4T7   705-324-6121
   From Peterborough, direct: 799-5201
   Emily: 705-799-5170
   Mark S. Burnham: District Office
   Peter's Woods: District Office
   Serpent Mounds: 705-295-6879

Otonabee Region Conservation Authority,
380 Armour Road, Time Square,
Peterborough, Ontario,
K9H 7L7   705-745-5791
For Heber Rogers, Hope Mill, Lang Mill,
Miller Creek, Selwyn, and Warsaw Caves.

Peterborough Centennial Museum and
Archives,
P.O. Box 143,
Peterborough, Ontario,
K9J 6Y5   705-743-5180

Peterborough Field Naturalists,
P.O. Box 1532,
Peterborough, Ontario,
K9J 7H7

Peterborough Information Centre,
229 King St.
For current telephone numbers
for the Astronomy Club, Rock
and Fossil Club, etc.   705-743-3166

Peterborough Kawartha Tourism and
Convention Bureau,
135 George St. North,
Peterborough, Ontario,
K9J 3G6   705-742-2201
                                 1-800-461-6424

Peterborough Public Library,
347 Alymer North,
Peterborough, Ontario   705-745-5382

Trent-Severn Waterway,
P.O. Box 567,
Peterborough, Ontario,
K9J 6Z6   705-742-9267

Trent University,
P.O. Box 4800,
Peterborough, Ontario,
K9J 7B8   705-748-1011

*Canoeists at
High Falls*

PHOTO CREDITS

Gordon Berry 31, 34, 39, 42, 56, 60, 74b, 76d, 80c,f, 81c, 102b,e, 106a,b
Rhea Bringeman 47
Les Brown 49b
Jim Buttle 14, 17
Terry Carpenter 8, 21a, 23, 28a, 98, 102a, 118
Geof Carpentier 28b, 57b, 63b, 80d,e, 81a,d, 106d
Fritz Clauer 6, 10, 55b, 61, 67, 93a
Mary Deacon 22, 27, 37, 46, 49a,b, 74e, 76b,c, 78, 96, 102d, 111
Jim Dunsire 63a, 91
John Fraser 33, 40
G. Henderson 32, 54, 55a, 68a, 73, 106c, 107, 112
Dudley Hewitt 45a, 74c
Conrad Hill 11, 41
Terry Hunter 50, 52a
Jack Lee 35, 85, 102c, 104

Jack Mark 120
Mike MacLean 79a,b, 99, 108a,b
Parks Canada 18
Don Porter 38, 81b, 92a, 97
Randy Romano 25, 71, 89
John Sadler 105
Phil Schappert 57a, 68b,c,d, 70a,b, 80a,b, 88
Wade Scorns 72a,b, 74d
Harry Williams 93b, 94a
G.R.C.A. 95, 101
K.R.C.A. 82a,b, 84, 86
M.N.R. 21b, 90, 92b, 110
O.R.C.A. 45b
P.F.N. 26, 43, 53, 64, 74a, 75, 81e, 94b
P.K. Tourism 28c, 66

Note: Letter references read left to right, top to bottom.

Luna moth